Life Beyond Life

Books by Hans Holzer

Non-Fiction

The Aquarian Age
Astrology: What It Can Do For You
Beyond Medicine
Beyond this Life
Charismatics
The Directory of the Occult
Elvis Presley Speaks (From the Beyond)
ESP and You
Ghost Hunter
Ghosts I've Met
The Ghosts that Walk in Washington
Gothic Ghosts
The Habsburg Curse
The Handbook of Parapsychology
Hans Holzer's Haunted Houses
Haunted Hollywood
Hidden Meanings in Dreams
Houses of Horror
How to Win at Life
The Human Dynamo
Inside Witchcraft
Life After Death: the Challenge and the Evidence
Murder in Amityville
Patterns of Destiny
Phantoms of Dixie
The Power of Hypnosis
The Powers of the New Age

The Primer of Reincarnation
The Prophets Speak
Psychic Healing
The Psychic Side of Dreams
Psycho-Ecstasy
Some of My Best Friends Are Ghosts
Speed Thinking
Star Ghosts
The Truth About ESP
The Truth About Witchcraft
The UFOnauts: New Facts on Extraterrestrial Landings
The Vegetarian Way of Life
Window to the Past
The Witchcraft Report
Yankee Ghosts
Where the Ghosts Are

Fiction

The Alchemist
The Alchemy Deception
The Amityville Curse
Circle of Love
The Clairvoyant
The Entry
Heather, Confessions of a Witch
The Red Chindvit Conspiracy
Star of Destiny
The Unicorn
The Zodiac Affairs

✳

Contents

✳
Preface

WE'VE COME A LONG WAY, I think, from those awkward jokes about coming back as ———, or of not wanting to hurt a fly because she may be someone's grandmother. The evidence for the existence of previous lives in all of us has mounted steadily over the past decade, and serious scientists like Dr. Ian Stevenson and Dr. Eugene Jussek have done convincing work in this field.

Reincarnation, then, is no longer a matter of belief or disbelief, like religion. It is a question of either accepting the *facts* pointing toward it or of rejecting them. Many people reject facts because they don't like what they imply. Lots of people live with a partial reality and do quite well in their lives because they keep away from controversy or anything that they do not wish to face. But the individual who has no such restrictions and who does have an objective interest in searching out the nature of man will sooner or later be confronted with material pertaining to the reincarnation questions and probably will have to take a position.

This is by no means easy; accepting the evidence for reincarnation, such as I am presenting it here, is not quite as inconsequential as accepting other evidence for anything of interest. If reincarnation is a fact, then it implies basic and profound involvement with the way we live, die, think, and act—in this life as well as the one following or the one that went before.

Only reincarnation offers a plausible explanation for the seeming inequities of this our physical world; only reincarnation gives us hope that we do have certain controls over an otherwise prearranged destiny: our behavior, our attitudes, our way of life . . . and afterlife.

Nothing stirs up more questions, nothing answers more questions, than the system of rebirth cycles in human existence. Those who will accept the system as natural and all-pervasive will find their lives falling into place differently than before: everything suddenly makes sense, everything moves as it ought to—even if some experiences are not pleasant—and there is frustration and pain mixed in with success and joy.

Nothing, either, exceeds the strength derived from one's understanding of the system—an understanding arrived at not on faith, on belief, on hearsay, but by reason of evaluating the existing evidence in a calm and objective manner.

To this purpose I am dedicating the present work, in the hope—nay, firm expectation—that it will help my reader come to terms with his or her existence in this state of consciousness.

Prof. Hans Holzer, Ph.D.

CHAPTER ONE

Introduction

THE PURPOSE OF THIS WORK is to acquaint my readers with new and unpublished material pointing in the direction of reincarnation, and to analyze this material in terms of some sort of system that would allow us to understand the phenomenon better than we have in the past. Furthermore, it is my intention to delineate a system under which reincarnation and karma seem to work. The purpose of this is to allow my readers to come to some conclusion concerning their philosophy of life; for it is my contention that the system involving reincarnation and the karmic law is the only plausible explanation for our world, the universe of which it is a part, and the seeming contradictions found therein.

As far back as the Stone Age, the ancient Celtic religion of witchcraft, or Wicca, held that man's ultimate goal is to return again and again in reincarnation cycles to fulfill that which he was unable to fulfill in an earlier lifetime.

Even Christianity, at least in its early forms, has overtones of rebirth, but we must speak of this at the proper time.

Reincarnation, then, as a subject at least in the Western world, somehow has always been linked with the East, and to this very day there are serious scientists who think that all examples of reincarnation, that is to say, all those cases that seem to have the ring of truth about them, must of necessity come from India or, at the very least, the East.

It will therefore come as a shock to those who think this way that not a single case in this book occurred in the Eastern part of the world, but, to the contrary, every single one is of Western origin, mainly American, recent, and of course factual as far as I am able to determine.

Religious philosophy has played absolutely no part in my work. The purpose of this book is not to reaffirm any religious concept but to determine by analysis whether reincarnation is a fact or a fallacy; to establish whether there are sufficient grounds, sufficient material and evidence, to support a conviction that people are reborn into other bodies, that life does not end at death's door but that all of us do return to continue the cycle of life and rebirth.

True, there are many books dealing with the subject, some of them in a philosophical manner, others quite factually; some of them were written quite recently. The problem, then, is not so much to write a book that will present facts never discussed before but to present them in such a manner that an open-minded person can accept them as true. By open-minded, I mean neither committed to reincarnation nor dead set against it. An open-minded person is one who has not yet made up his mind and who is willing to examine the evidence at face value.

The difficulty is not only of defining what reincarnation is, but also what constitutes *proof* of reincarnation. First of all, reincarnation is not a return in an animal's body but in human form. This may occur at various times in one's life cycle, and it does not follow that everyone reincarnates in exactly the same manner. Far from it! The variety of reincarnation material suggests that each case is different and must, therefore, be examined on its own merits.

To define my quest, then, scientifically, I would say first that reincarnation is the return of a human being in another life. Proof must be of a kind that cannot be explained away by ordinary means. It cannot be vague or subject to another explanation, such as having read books dealing with a particular period or knowledge of the person one feels one has come back as because of some family connection. All these things have to be taken into account when one weighs the evidence, of course; for proof must be absolute, or reasonably absolute. Man is fallible, and nothing is one hundred percent correct in our lives, but one must strive to attain at least a reasonable amount of evidence before one accepts reincarnation as a fact.

Reincarnation, if generally accepted as factual, would, of course, greatly influence our personal conduct. I am referring especially to the conduct in times of war, under conditions of violence, or whenever there is a possibility of taking another person's life. Whenever a man or a woman is faced with the commission of a crime or an evil deed (I mean evil in terms of contemporary morality), there is the possibility of "accumulating karma"; that is to say, of mortgaging one's future lifetime in a negative sense. Now, if reincarnation is subject to a universal law of retribution and justice, then an evil deed committed in one lifetime may very well have dire consequences in the next one. The knowledge of this might influence people toward a better life, toward a more moral existence. It may prevent crimes of violence, perhaps even war. This may only be wishful thinking on my part, but it stands to reason that a universal and scientifically accepted conviction that reincarnation is factual would have deep and long-lasting consequences in our entire way of life. The common attitude toward death, for instance, would undergo rapid and profound changes, for if there is more than one lifetime to live, surely one would not fear death as the inevitable end. One might even welcome it at times if the existence one suffers could be exchanged for a better one within a short time. The hopelessly ill might very well welcome the continuing life cycle.

Let there be no mistake about this: Reincarnation is a very important subject today. It may very well be the most important subject tomorrow.

CHAPTER TWO

What Exactly *Is* Reincarnation?

WHAT EXACTLY IS REINCARNATION? Dervied from the Latin, *reincarnation* literally means "to enter the flesh again." The equivalent term in German, *Wiederverkörperung*, means reembodiment. Other descriptive terms include *rebirth, to be born again*, in German, *Wiedergeburt* (rebirth). In French, the word *renaissance* has the same literal meaning (rebirth) but is not used in the same way. Renaissance simply means a renewal of life or interest in life; a rebirth of productivity. Capitalized, it refers to renewed interest in classical art. The number of incarnations is not defined in any term; it merely indicates that one has been born at some other time.

In the world of parapsychology we speak of discarnates and incarnates, meaning dead individuals and living individuals. A reincarnated individual has been born again in a physical body, with the understanding that some sort of memory or proof lingers on from that earlier lifetime. Basically, the idea of reincarnation involves the conviction that one may die and lose one's physical body and then return in another physical body, live another lifetime, and, presumably, die again in the same manner only to return once again for any number of times. This system involves either no memory of previous lives or only partial memory of the so-called karmic law governing it. Of this more later. Reincarnation concepts should not be mistaken for two other ideas with which they are frequently confused. *Anabaptism*, meaning to be baptized again, is

4

purely a religious concept prevalent among certain Protestant splinter groups. In the sixteenth century a group of religious fanatics called Anabaptists even seized the city of Münster in Westphalia and held it for awhile, establishing a religiously oriented state. This state was eventually destroyed by the Bishop of Münster, and the Anabaptists were mercilessly suppressed. The French composer Giacomo Meyerbeer wrote a celebrated opera, *Le Prophete*, based on this event.

In more recent times, certain American Fundamentalist communities have also practiced Anabaptism. The idea behind it is to be baptized again, usually after one has reached adulthood, as a declaration of faith in Jesus Christ; the original baptism, undertaken when the subject was a mere baby and therefore unable to grasp the significance of the act, is thus reinforced by a conscious baptism at a time when the individual is fully aware of the implications, and thus can make his declaration of faith that much stronger.

Another idea frequently confused with reincarnation is *transmigration,* which refers to the passing of the soul from one state to another at death. Actually, to transmigrate means to journey through an area. Transmigration signifies a possible incarnation of a human soul into animal form and, conversely, the rebirth of an animal soul into a human at a later stage of development in order to purify the soul. This philosophy, basically of oriental origin, is based on the idea that all life must undergo a gradual development up the ladder of existence. It was part and parcel of the Egyptian religion in antiquity; it is still considered a valid belief by the Vedic religion of present-day India. To date I have not found any strictly scientific evidence to support this contention. This does not mean that the concept is impossible, it only means that no factual evidence has yet turned up to support it. Probably the most valid parallel to the concept of transmigration can be found by observing the stages of the human fetus. It undergoes a rapid passing through various stages of development, including a number of animal stages. Some warm-blooded animals also undergo changes from a lower order of existence to the final, higher state into which they are born. No doubt future research will enlighten us further on this aspect of soul travel.

Reincarnation has always been viewed differently in the West than in the East. By West I mean Europe and the Americas—to the extent that they were colonized by European people. By East I mean Near, Middle, and Far East and Africa. Western society, being more rationally inclined due to genetic and environmental conditions, has in modern time generally viewed reincarnation as a subject not fit for logical discussion. Only in recent years has it become fashionable in the West to consider the possibility on a scientific basis. Western civilization, therefore, has nearly always avoided considering the impact of such a system upon its development. When there was material pointing in the direction of reincarnation, it was considered an oddity or an exception to an otherwise perfect system. If avoidance did not lead to a total sweeping under the carpet, then the problem of explaining the "unusual phenomenon" of reincarnation was relegated to religious and philosophical authorities. Most of the great philosophers of the nineteenth century viewed reincarnation with little respect. Even in our century, men who were friendly toward psychical research, like Dr. Carl Jung, did not go far enough in accepting the probability of reincarnation. If anything, the idea of "coming back as someone else" was a subject for popular jokes; in particular, the idea of coming back as an animal was held up as punishment for misdeeds in another lifetime.

A kind of transmigration is a frequent subject in Western mythology and in the wider realm of fairy stories. The idea of the enchanted prince who must live as a frog until some fair maiden saves him from his fate by being faithful runs through most Western societies. But the change from one form of existence to another was not a matter of advancing development. Rather, it was a fiat of some supernatural authority, such as a sorcerer or a deity. Changing a human being into an animal or vice versa was reserved to those possessed of magical or superior powers.

No attempt at verification was ever made of these myths and stories. The stories were taken at face value by children but regarded as symbolic or merely charming tales by adults. One might possibly consider them as indicative of turning the inner man into something more valuable, but I doubt that many adults look at fairy tales with such far-reaching and analytical eyes. The idea of changing a human being into something else or an animal into a human being is not so much an expression of the desirability of the altered state as an expression of power; that is, the power of the one who does the enchanting. Sometimes the power to change is inherent in the position the sorcerer holds. A great magician, a wise man, a powerful king perhaps are expected to have inherent powers to do all sorts of wondrous things. An evil witch—standard character of the Western European fairy tale—also has the power to do terrible things to human beings and to animals. In her case, the power comes with the job. Others may obtain the power temporarily or on special occasions: the little boy who overhears a gnome speak the magical formula that opens the mountain, imitates it, and also succeeds only to be tripped up later by the very fact that his magical knowledge is incomplete. Or the power may be conferred on an ordinary mortal by a superior agency, such as the good fairy granting someone three wishes. In most fairy tales, magical formulas or words are used. The power inherent in *words* goes back to the very dawn of mankind, when nearly all religions considered the name of the deity sacred and possessed of great powers. In pronouncing the name of the deity (or deities) in vain, that power was dissipated, and consequently the name was not spoken but covered up by the use of another term. Word magic rests largely on the belief that it works; changing from one appearance to another—from human being to animal and vice versa—is possible instantaneously, provided one knows the right words. They have to be spoken in just the right way or at a certain time or in a special place, of course. Ancient magical manuscripts supplied the necessary details. In many fairy tales such special books form part of the lore.

Although the concept of transmigration as such is not anchored in Western philosophy, the idea that one might change shape under special circumstances runs through all of it. In addition to the fairy tale, there are of course the horror tales, such as the werewolf traditions of Eastern Europe, and vampirism, said to originate in Romania but also strongly entrenched in Western Europe. According to these beliefs, man can change into a wolf or vampire—a blood-sucking animal—at certain times, especially when the moon is full. Actually, *lycanthropy* is a real disease, in which an individual displays animalistic behavior due to certain disturbances of the nervous and vascular systems.

In the East, the idea of transmigration is much more firmly

anchored. Even with religions in which it does not form part of the dogma, the idea of being changed into an animal at the discretion of the Supreme Power occurs from time to time. Messengers from heaven or hell or their equivalents appear in various disguises and are capable of changing back and forth with the greatest of ease. Anyone who has ever read the *Arabian Nights* knows of the jins, or little devils, and of course of the genie, another form of the same word. In the Tibetan pantheon alone there are several hundred demons or demigods, many of them part animal or all animal in appearance and representing various forces of nature. Similar interweaving of the worlds of man and of animals occurs in the Vedic religion. Animalistic forms occur on occasions in Buddhism and Shintoism as well. However, there is no well-ordered system whereby every soul goes through various states—from low animal to human being and beyond into a divine form of existence—such as we find, for instance, in the ancient Egyptian religion. Orthodox Hindus holds such beliefs, it is true, but the caste system is still tied to individual effort and does not work equally for everybody. Just the same, in the Vedic religion we have the closest approach to orderly belief in reincarnation as we understand it in terms of Western research. Although the Hindu accepts reincarnation as part of his religion, and on faith alone, it gives him the same comfort a Westerner might derive from scientific evidence pointing to the existence of the reincarnation for all.

In the East, especially in Africa, we find the belief in the return of souls into the bodies of their own descendants, such as the souls of important warriors or kings returning in the bodies of their children. These beliefs are not based on any objective research but are more in the nature of political stratagems. Similarly, the Tibetan search for the next incarnation of the Dalai Lama immediately following the death of the previous Dalai Lama is motivated not so much by objective research methods as by considerations of state and religious beliefs.

When we leave the area of religion and philosophy, where, after all, everyone may have his own ideas—ideas with which one can scarcely argue since they are essentially personal—we come face to face with the public acceptance of, and attitude toward, the reported occurrences of seemingly valid reincarnation cases. In the East, such matters are still reported in the press and in books with very little public attention, almost with public apathy. This isn't because the public lacks interest in such matters but because, by and large, the people of the East have lived with the concept of reincarnation, and frequently also of transmigration, for so long that any reports bearing on such subjects seem anticlimactic to them. Only among revolutionary societies and certain government circles in present-day India do we find active resistance to reports dealing with reincarnation material. But even in modern India, there are several universities studying phenomena of this kind in much the same way universities study them in the West; Professor H. N. Banerjee is probably the best-known authority in this area.

Although the Soviet Union and her satellites have until recently looked with jaundiced eyes upon all psychical phenomena, research projects into ESP phenomena and all related subjects are now going on at more than a dozen universities in the Communist states. When reincarnation material occurs, it is treated with respect, although they do not necessarily reach the same conclusions a Western researcher might.

But in the free West, which includes, as I have already pointed-ed out, the Americas, reincarnation as a serious public issue dates back only a few years. True, Swedish researchers regressed subjects with excellent results many years before the Bridey Murphy case burst upon the public scene. But it was Morey Bernstein, with his book *The Search for Bridey Murphy*, who acquainted large sectors of the general public with evidential material pertaining to reincarnation.

Bernstein is the son of a wealthy manufacturer of plumbing, heating, and electrical supplies in Pueblo, Colorado. In 1953 he became interested in hypnosis and started to experiment with various subjects. As a young man of means, he did this solely out of curiosity and not because he hoped that his research would yield anything of commercial value. In his home in Colorado, and later in New York City, he pursued his studies of hypnosis and regression into former lives with a zeal that overshadowed all his other duties. Shortly after Bernstein concluded his first experiments with a housewife from Colorado, Mrs. Virginia Tighe, now known as Mrs. Morrow, Bernstein played the tapes for me in his New York City apartment. I was impressed with both the sincerity of his efforts and the quality of the tapes, which contained much regression material concerning an alleged former life of Mrs. Tighe in Ireland.

Under hypnotic regression, Mrs. Tighe recalled in great detail her life as Bridget, or Bridey, Murphy, giving so much in the way of names, dates, and places (Bridey Murphy was born in Cork in 1798 and died in Belfast in 1864) that Bernstein felt sure he had stumbled upon an authentic case of reincarnation. He told his findings for the first time in the *Empire Magazine,* the magazine supplement of the *Denver Post,* in 1954. The response to his article was so great that he decided to put it all into book form, and, in 1956, *The Search for Bridey Murphy* was published. In the book, he protected Mrs. Tighe by giving her anonymity. This was a wise move since the book became an immediate best-seller. Despite the attempt to hide her name from public knowledge, entrepreneurs managed to get through to Mrs. Tighe and offered her all sorts of opportunities, ranging from nightclub appearances to franchising automobile agencies. Despite the documented findings, however, Mrs. Tighe does not believe in reincarnation to this day. Both she and Mr. Bernstein refused all kinds of offers, preferring the rational, scientific approach to the problem. They did, however, permit Paramount to make a movie based on the book. In the motion picture Teresa Wright played Mrs. Tighe and Louis Hayward, Bernstein. Part of the payment received for the motion picture rights went to the subject. The motion picture was a flop, perhaps because it treated the book with less than sincerity and respect.

Today, if you were to ask the average person whether he remembers Bridey Murphy, most likely he would answer, "Yes, but wasn't that proved to be a hoax?" This, if nothing else, proves the old Roman saying *semper aliquid haeret,* meaning "something always sticks." No matter how great a lie or smear, no matter how unfounded, people will remember it even if it has later been proven false. Thus it was with the book. Although it is not generally known, a major picture magazine tried to buy rights to the story from Mr. Bernstein. The author did not like the terms and refused the offer. Shortly afterward, the same picture magazine sent a team of investigators to look into the background of Mrs. Tighe. In the Middle West they came up with what they claimed to be proof of Mrs. Tighe's Irish background. From bits and pieces, neighborhood conversations, hasty conclusions concerning her acquaintanceship with an Irish priest, the picture magazine constructed the story that the "reincarnation memory" was actually due to her childhood memories of Irish people in her immediate environment. So contrived was this "explanation," and so patently motivated by the earlier rejection of a sale to the same magazine, that Mr. Berstein's hometown paper—the respected *Denver Post*—found the money and personnel to put together an investigative team of their own. The *Denver Post* team, however, went all the way to Ireland to check out the original story in painstaking detail. The result was that the *Denver Post* published a six-part series concerning the Bridey Murphy case, in which not only were all of Mr. Bernstein's original findings corroborated but much new material was added to it, upholding the reincarnation theory.

Later on, the new material was incorporated into a reissue of the book itself and in the paperback version, which came out in 1970. At that time, Morey Bernstein spent part of the year in Miami. As a result of the renewed interest in the story, Bernstein and his star subject were interviewed again in the press and on television. "Writing *Bridey* was the most important thing I've done in my lifetime," Bernstein was quoted as saying. "Today the book is taken seriously by psychic researchers and enjoying a new popularity. It has been called a parapsychological classic, and its principals are finally able to laugh at its debunkers," says Bob Wilcox, the *Miami News* religion editor. Nowadays, Morey Bernstein commutes between his winter home in Colorado and his summer home in Florida, is knee-deep in the investment business, and is planning to write two more books.

CHAPTER THREE

The Scientific View
of Reincarnation

"THE EVIDENCE INDICATES that reincarnation is a fact. I think it likely that people have been born before and that after they die will be born again on this earth." This is the headline-making quotation in an article on reincarnation in the popular weekly, *The National Enquirer*. This weekly newspaper is not known for its subtlety of approach, nor for the reliability of its information. But in recent times the *Enquirer* has abandoned a hardcore policy of scandal and violence for a large percentage of headline-making news from the field of parapsychology, astrology, and the occult in general. As a result, its circulation has risen to even greater heights than before.

The above quotation is not from some metaphysical believer or astrologer or amateur investigator. It is the expressed opinion of Dr. Ian Stevenson, head of the Department of Neurology and Psychiatry at the University of Virginia's School of Medicine. Dr. Stevenson has for many years been the champion of reincarnation research in the United States. His first book on the subject, *Twenty Cases Suggestive of Reincarnation,* was soon followed by additional material that he published through the American Society for Psychical Research. Stevenson has investigated cases both in the West and in the East and has done so on a careful, scientific basis. No one can rightly accuse Dr. Stevenson of being a charlatan or of jumping to conclusions. His language is careful, and he makes no unjustified claims. The difficulty toward total acceptance of his findings and the findings of others like myself that parallel them lies in the stubborn insistence on the part of most orthodox scientists that laboratory experiments are the only way of proving reincarnation. "Nobody has as yet thought up a way that reincarnation could be proved in a laboratory or a test tube," the professor is quoted in his interview. In studying hundreds of valid reincarnation cases, he had combined the methods of the historian, lawyer, and psychiatrist. Gathering testimony from as many witnesses as he could, he and his staff sometimes interviewed as many as twenty-five people regarding a certain case. Sometimes, if the original talk has not been satisfactory or conclusive, he goes back for further interviews. Everything is taken into account: the behavior of the person who claims to have lived before; the environment in which he lives; his background, education, and general knowledge; and even his personal habits. "Many of those claiming to have lived before are children. Often they are very emotional when they talk of the person they used to be, and they can give minute details of the life they lived," Dr. Stevenson added.

Dr. Stevenson, just as any responsible parapsychologist, always looks for alternate explanations so that he may rule them out, before he accepts reincarnation as the answer to a puzzling case. Everything is considered: early experiences, accidental information, newspaper accounts—anything that might have been forgotten consciously but can be brought out under hypnosis. Fraud, memory lapses, fantasy, and wishful thinking are considered and eventually ruled out before a valid case for reincarnation is established, according to Dr. Stevenson's method of inquiry. But that is by no means the end. He explained that he also considers and excludes telepathy as a means of obtaining unusual information. "Extrasensory perception cannot account for the fact that the subject has skills and talents not learned, such as the ability to speak a foreign language without having had the opportunity to learn it in this present life."

Although most of the cases investigated by Dr. Stevenson were in India and the East, he has also looked into some interesting situations in Alaska and Europe. This is not because fewer cases occur in the West but because the prevailing attitude of the public makes discovery of such cases more difficult. In the East, the climate is more favorable toward a free and open discussion of such matters; in the West, only very courageous people dare come out with statements that they may have lived before.

Old-line scientists prefer to regard reincarnation research as exotic and reject the evidence out of hand without ever examining it. Some parapsychologists, even conservative ones, are eager to examine the material there is, especially since Dr. Stevenson has opened the door to such investigations. The acceptance of reincarnation as a reality is a hard nut to swallow for some. Inevitably, it also means acceptance of survival after physical death. Some parapsychologists still cannot accept that probability simply because they have been weaned on laboratory research methods and cannot or do not wish to understand that the evidence is in the field among spontaneous phenomena or actual, unplanned occurrences.

The material for the survival of human personality is overwhelming, far more so than the evidence for reincarnation. Strangely, though, some support for reincarnation research can be gotten among scientists who, on the surface, would be the least likely to be interested in such a subject. I am speaking here of physicists and physical scientists. The reason is that in learning about the nature of energy and mass, and in dealing with the electromagnetic forces in the universe, many of these scientists have come to realize that energy is indestructible. Basing their views to some extent on Albert Einstein's pioneering opinions, they, too, feel that energy may be transformed into other forms of power or into mass but can never be dissipated entirely. Since the life force—the human personality—is an energy field, they argue that such fields cannot be dissipated either and must therefore *continue to exist in some form*. Experiments involving the discovery of energy fields in so-called haunted locations and of significant changes in the atmosphere of an experimental chamber, such as ionization, have been going on for some time. It is therefore not too surprising that such strong centers of technical learning as the Newark College of Engineering and the New York Institute of Technology (where I teach) should be interested in parapsychology and, within that field, reincarnation research.

Medical science has been more hostile toward reincarnation material than any other branch of science. This may be due to the fact that medical science relies heavily upon the assumption that man is essentially a physical being. As Dr. William McGary, the brilliant physician working in conjunction with the Association for Research and Enlightenment in Phoenix, Arizona, has pointed out to me, on a recent visit, that the basic difference between orthodox medical science and medicine based upon such knowledge as the Edgar Cayce records lies in the way they regard the human being. To conventional medicine, man is structural; that is to say, the physical body is the essence of man and mind is merely a subdivision thereof. To the esoterically oriented person, man is functional, not structural. The physical person is a manifestation of spirit, or mind which came first, and represents the outward expression of the soul that governs and determines everything from within. Such thinking is at variance with conventional medical procedure, of course, since it necessitates the treating of illness from a total point of view rather than from the usual sectional or physical viewpoint.

For a medical doctor to accept reincarnation as a reality requires changes in his medical approach as well; except for the psychiatrist, the conventional physician has little to do with the nonphysical aspects of human personality. The general practitioner and the specialist both leave mental problems to the psychiatrist, concentrating on purely physical problems. Thus the question of reincarnation research becomes essentially one of acceptance or rejection by the psychiatrist and psychoanalyst. Today, the majority of psychiatrists explain any valid reincarnation material as malfunctions of personality, ranging all the way from mild neuroses to schizophrenic conditions. Just as the conventional analyst will regard *all* dream material of his patient as purely symbolic and representative of suppressed material in the unconscious part of the mind, so the psychiatrist will explain reincarnation memories either as aberrations of the mind or, if the particular psychiatrist is a Jungian, as racial memories, or archetypes.

But these scoffing psychiatrists and analysts seem to forget that Dr. Sigmund Freud, the father of modern psychiatry, himself leaned toward parapsychology in the later years of his life. He made the statement in print that he would want to study parapsychology if he had to do it all over again. One of his star pupils, Dr. Carl Jung, who has contributed as much to psychiatry as Freud, was not only firmly convinced of the reality of psychic phenomena but possessed ESP himself. His discovery or, if you prefer, invention of the *archetypes* as a symbolic expression of "original concepts" does not militate against genuine reincarnation experiences, in his view. At the Jung Institute in Zurich, much research went on in this area in the 1930s and 1940s. In his important work *Acausal Synchronicity (The Law of Meaningful Coincidence)* Jung postulates that there is a superior order of things connecting events and people. This superior order lies beyond the law of cause and effect and must be dealt with on different terms. What Jung is hinting at in this precedent-shaking work is the existence of a law of fate; by trying to explore the ways in which this noncausal link seemed to work, Jung approached the question of fate, free will, and reincarnation (which is intimately connected with them) in a modern, scientific way for the first time.

⁂

CHAPTER FOUR

The Religious View
of Reincarnation

THE RELIGIOUS ESTABLISHMENT has viewed reincarnation with various attitudes. In the past, any deviation from the norm was considered heresy. People were persecuted for it more in the West than in the East, but, in essence, no established churches like their followers to have doctrinal ideas of their own. In the West, early Christianity contained elements of beliefs in reincarnation. This may be due to the Essene influences that showed in the teachings of Jesus, due to his background as a student at the Essene monastery at Quumram.

When Christianity became a state religion and the early concepts were edited to fit in with this new view of the faith, much early material was deliberately omitted or suppressed. Not only were several books of the Bible removed, but also passages intimating belief in reincarnation were taken out or rewritten in subsequent translations. From about 300 A.D. onward, Christianity was no longer identical with the early teachings of Jesus but had become a combination of his teachings with later religious philosophical thought and the necessities of an emerging state religion. The Medieval Church had no use for reincarnation. Belief in the Final Judgment, a moment when the dead are called to account for their sins on earth, is a cornerstone of Christian dogma. If man were to go through a succession of lives without that Final Judgment Day, much of the power of the faith would have been lost. The Church needed the whip of Judgment Day to keep the faithful in line. It was therefore a matter of survival for the Church not to allow belief in reincarnation to take hold among her followers.

For somewhat different reasons, the Jewish religion does not like the idea of reincarnation either, even though there are hints of it in Scriptures. Notably, the Prophet Elijah was always expected to come again, and this idea can even be found in early Christianity. But the Hebrew faith rejected the idea of reincarnation, since it would indicate a system that was not wholly dependent upon the grace and will of a merciful God. A personal God was very much at the heart of both Hebrew and Christian faiths in the beginning. Only in later years did the moral concept of religion become a stronger focal point.

Some Protestant faiths, especially the Fundamentalists emphasized Jesus Christ as the personal savior of mankind. Consequently, a law that applies universally to all men and gives them rebirth regardless of this personal savior is particularly odious to the Fundamentalists.

Some great religious leaders say one thing but their followers understand another. Emanuel Swedenborg was an eighteenth-century scientist, philosopher, and seer in Sweden. Among his proven accomplishments is a detailed description of the great fire of Stockholm, which he described to a number of witnesses while some seventy miles away. Swedenborg did not found a new religion in his lifetime; his many books, among which *Heaven and Hell* is perhaps the best known, were later used as the foundation for a religious faith called simply The New Church. It has many followers in Scandinavian countries and in this country, especially in Minnesota, where many immigrants from Northern Europe settled, but also in various other parts of the United States. A cornerstone of this religion is a belief in the coming of a "New Jerusalem."

The writings of Swedenborg indicate quite clearly that he had visions in which he saw "the other side of life" very much the way spiritualists do and almost the same way scientists feel who follow the "survivalist" line in parapsychology. The terminology may differ but, in essence, Swedenborg spoke of a number of "societies" where people live after physical death. Depending upon the state of consciousness prior to death, one joins a particular society and advances to a higher one when one is ready to do so. The Sweden-borgians in the United States are, by and large, a peaceful lot and not given to missionary efforts. It was therefore with some surprise that I received a note from Duncan Brackin of Minneapolis, an avid Swedenborgian, wondering how I could possibly lean toward rein-carnation. "Swedenborg proved reincarnation to be an error once and for all for those who have eyes to see," Mr. Brackin com-plained. He sent me a little pamphlet entitled *Reincarnation—The View of The New Church.* As far as rebirth is concerned, the Swedenborgian church accepts only spiritual rebirth, and that dur-ing the earthly life of man and mostly while man is not even aware of it.

Among modern churches, the Episcopal Church and some of the liberal Christian churches, such as the Universalist and Uni-tarian faiths, have been most receptive to material hinting at the reality of reincarnation. They see no conflict of insurmountable proportions in the teaching of reincarnation and their own con-cepts. As long as man accepts the teachings of Jesus, they feel that it does not matter whether he lived once or several times. Very few Catholic priests and laymen will commit themselves on the subject of reincarnation. Those who are open-minded toward it are quite unusual. The problem here lies with fundamental issues: if psychic phenomena are accepted as natural and realistic happenings, the entire basis of the miraculous story of Jesus could be explained entirely on the basis of psychical research. This would, on the other hand, make the miraculous side of it far more acceptable to sophisticated individuals who do not accept their religion on faith alone. But, on the other hand, it would deprive the account of the Resurrection of its uniqueness. It is precisely that uniqueness that the Church needs so sorely to build her entire edifice upon.

Nothing reported about Jesus, both while in the body and after his physical death, is inconsistent with the findings of modern parapsychology. As a matter of fact, parallel happenings have been reported from many other quarters. Perhaps none of them were quite as spectacular or had such fortuitous dissemination, but psy-chical healing, materialization and dematerialization, levitation, and finally, the appearance of a person known to have died after physical death are well-attested phenomena that have occurred, from time to time, in the annals of psychical research all over the world. What makes the position of Jesus unique, therefore, is not the phenomena as such but the *implication* of the phenomena and, of course, Jesus' teachings and views. The phenomena themselves, in my opinion, were used by Jesus consciously and deliberately to underscore his belief in the continuance of life after death. Whether Jesus was, in fact, a believer in reincarnation cannot be ascertained with certainty, especially since so many of his sayings and teachings have been lost, or were perhaps eliminated at later dates. But there was a belief among Jesus' contemporaries that he had come as the reincarnated Prophet Elijah, and a much-quoted exhortation, "to live, you must be born again" may be a hint at reincarnation beliefs. Much of Jesus' philosophy was misunderstood even at the time when he promulgated it. His references to his "Father," his assertion that his Kingdom was not of this world, "judge not lest ye be judged," are all indications of symbolic language and were, I think, not to be taken literally.

Although we are moving toward greater enlightenment in religion and a much more flexible attitude on the part of the various religious establishments, we have as yet not come to grips with the problem of integrating scientific findings into the religious edifice, especially when such findings go counter to traditional doctrine. When the various religious establishments realize that there lies strength in incorporating scientifically supported findings of this kind into their philosophies, they may very well regain their following, especially among the young.

※

CHAPTER FIVE

Regressive Hypnosis as Evidence for Reincarnation

To BEGIN WITH, no one should undertake regression experiments unless he or she is fully qualified to do so. By qualified I mean not simply a knowledge of hypnosis—that, of course, is necessary—but also I mean a deeper understanding of the problems involved in bringing a person back, through childhood and the threshold of birth, into an earlier lifetime. Only a trained psychic researcher and hypnotist should undertake this.

When *The Search for Bridey Murphy* was a best-seller, a great deal of attention was focused on this technique. Morey Bernstein had come to the field as a novice, and hypnosis to him was nothing more than a hobby at first. That his book was honest and authentic is the more to his credit. Despite those who tried to discredit it, it was later fully exonerated. But there is the danger when those unfamiliar with the technique are involving themselves with it that a person may have unresolved psychiatric problems in this lifetime that can become acute or aggravated by simple hypnosis. If such is the case, the operator—that is to say, the hypnotist—must be qualified to deal with them so that no damage may result to the psyche of the subject.

Assuming, then, that those who wish to regress another person are fully qualified to undertake this task, I will proceed to explain the techniques I find most useful and successful in obtaining the desired information.

To begin with, the majority of individuals who feel they might be good subjects generally are not. Just because someone claims that hypnosis would yield good results with him or her doesn't mean that this will be the case. Many people harbor resentments and other forms of resistance, usually on an unconscious level. They cannot be hypnotized even though consciously they are willing to go under the hypnotist's spell.

I find that no more than one fourth of those who are willing subjects can actually be brought under hypnotic control, and only one in ten people make excellent hypnotic subjects. There is no rule as to the kind of person who can be easily hypnotized. Generally, women are easier to hypnotize than men. But even among women there are exceptions, for hysterical conditions may very well prevent them from letting go control over their bodies and personalities, something absolutely essential if genuine hypnosis is to take place. Emotional people are probably more prone to be good subjects than logical and reserved individuals.

A positive attitude toward the experiment is valuable but not essential. On the other hand, a negative attitude, which includes unwillingness to let go of one's self-control, may frequently thwart the efforts of the operator. I usually suggest that the subject make himself or herself comfortable on a couch or in an easy chair, remove shoes if they are too confining, and relax for a few moments before beginning the actual verbalization. I then suggest that the person close his or her eyes and listen to my voice. I will usually count from one to ten and suggest that at the count of ten the person be fully relaxed. This is followed by instructions to the various limbs of the person's body, saying that the limbs are becoming heavier and heavier, and that the whole body finally feels as if it were sinking down into the couch.

I then proceed to suggest that the individual is quite alone and can only hear my voice coming to him or her from a distance, but that no extraneous noises will be heard by him or her. Again I count to ten, suggesting that at the end of the second ten the individual will float out into the distance, far away from his or her usual surroundings, but that my voice will always be heard.

Depending on the success of the first stage, I then suggest that the individual will be able to hear everything I say and will not awaken until I awaken him or her; that, however, he or she will answer all my questions without awakening.

All this time I observe very closely and carefully whether hypnosis is in fact taking place or whether the person is still fully awake. I do not test my subjects with needles or in any other physical manner. This is strictly for stage hypnotists, and I view their work with both alarm and disdain, for hypnosis is too serious a subject to be used for entertainment purposes.

To reach the third or deepest stage of hypnosis I will suggest another ten steps down an imaginary staircase, toward the sea or toward some pleasant open area such as a meadow. I suggest conditions symbolizing freedom from all problems, total aloneness and a happy climate such as a blue sky, clouds overhead, a sunny day, or some other form of atmospheric condition symbolic of well-being. At this point, most subjects are indeed under hypnotic control. I test this by asking the individual for his or her name and age, and if he or she is not hypnotized at this point I will be told, "But I am not under yet, Mr. Holzer." In that event I have to start all over again, and if I do not succeed the second time, I generally dismiss the subject and ask him or her to return some other time, for it can very well happen that a subject feels tense on first meeting me and may be relaxed a second time. If after the second visit no hypnosis results, I regretfully dismiss the subject and turn to another person for further research.

No one can be hypnotized against his will or without his express wish to go under—at least not in the total sense in which I use hypnosis. People have fallen under spells through repetition, through advertising, or through slogans that they may hear or see on such mass communication media as television or the stage. But specific personal hypnosis, especially the kind needed for regression, is possible only with the cooperation of the subject.

Assuming that my subject has now gone down to the third, or deepest, stage of hypnosis, I will suggest age regression. This means that I will say, you are now so many years old and so many years old, and gradually will suggest the person is at a younger and earlier period in his or her life. Having suggested a specific date in the person's lifetime, I will then request information about the circumstances he or she lived under at that time. I will ask for the name of a schoolteacher or an address where the person and his or her parents lived at the time, the sort of information that only a person would know if he or she were indeed at that age, and the kind of information that one is prone to forget at a later stage in life. This, of course, proves that under hypnosis one remembers a great deal more than one is aware of in the conscious, or ordinary, state.

Gradually, I will then regress the person back to childhood and to the moment of birth. After this I suggest that he or she cross the threshold of birth into another lifetime. Sometimes I will give a figure, such as fifty years before your birth or a hundred years before your birth; or at other times I will simply direct the person to go back until he or she meets an earlier incarnation, until he or she comes up to another person in another lifetime. When this happens, I ask for specific details and a description of the person, the period, and the circumstances under which the scenes now described take place.

Having obtained information of this kind, I will then bring the individual back into the present by easy stages, making sure that he or she is not taken out of the hypnotic stage too quickly. Just before bringing him or her back to ordinary consciousness, I will suggest that nothing be remembered from the discussion or conversation held between myself and the subject under hypnosis. I will then add that a feeling of well-being will be experienced immediately upon awakening. If the individual has requested that I help him or her fight against abuses or bad habits, such as excessive smoking or drinking, I will at that moment insert a message to the unconscious to the effect that the person will not be able to smoke or drink as much as before, or not at all, depending upon the desire of the individual. After that, I will count to ten once again, instructing the individual that at the second count of ten, he or she will be fully awake and in good spirits.

This happens quickly, and the individual generally does not remember much or anything of the conversation that has taken place between us while under hypnotic regression. If some parts are remembered, this indicates that hypnosis was not as deep as desirable and that on future occasions I must correct this condition. However, even a full remembrance of everything said under hypnosis does not prove that the state of hypnotic regression was not in fact successful. Some individuals have total recall even when instructed not to do so.

A few minutes later, the subject will be allowed to get up and go home. Generally, I need between one and five sessions to establish full character in the case of previous lifetimes. On occasion, a single session has done what four or five sessions might do in other cases. This all depends on the depth at which the earlier lifetime material is buried in the unconscious of the subject.

I never do any corroboration or research while still working actively with a subject but begin my conscious research only after I am satisfied that I have obtained all the possible material that I can from this particular subject.

There is, of course, the problem of fantasy, which one must always reckon with. Some researchers feel that reincarnation material in general consists only of fantasy manufactured by a willing unconscious to please the researcher. I do not for a moment accept this version, but there are cases where fantasy may play a part. However, in my many years of reincarnation research, I have never encountered a seemingly genuine case where fantasy played a significant role, but I have encountered cases of hypnosis in which subjects related fantasy stories in order to work out some depressed material or some unattainable goal in real life. These, however, pertain solely to the present incarnation and not to earlier lifetimes.

When dealing with genuine or seemingly genuine material, it is always imperative to try to corroborate as much of it as possible. Only when at least a portion of the information can be traced and is not due to other factors can we assume reincarnation to be the explanation. Then, too, we must realize that reincarnation does not work, apparently, in the same way for everybody; and that it is a highly individual and sophisticated process in which each case must be taken on its own merits. There are rules, but they do not apply to everyone in exactly the same way. How the law works is still partially a mystery, but that it *exists*, I do not doubt in the least.

※

CHAPTER SIX

Recurrent Dreams Indicative of Reincarnation

SINCE MAN'S UNCONSCIOUS MIND can be entered more easily during the sleeping state, a large number of psychic experiences take place while the individual is asleep. It appears that the communications, such as they may be, can be implanted in the unconscious of the sleeper with less resistance from the conscious mind than would be the case if the communication were attempted during a wakeful state.

The majority of dreams, however, do not fall into this category. There are four different types of dreams: The first type of dream may be caused by physical discomfort; the second type may contain suppressed emotional material, frequently of a symbolic nature and furnishing the basic material for the psychoanalyst; a third type of dream contains psychic material if the individual is sufficiently advanced in his or her ESP development; and the fourth type of dream corresponds to what is now called "out of the body" experience in which the etheric body of the individual travels to places outside of the physical body. Recurrent dreams fall into the third category and consist of precise, frequently emotionally tinged dreams that repeat identical or very similar scenes more than one time. The more frequently the recurrent dream occurs, the stronger the emotional memory seems to be. This does not mean that potential reincarnation material cannot also be found in single dreams; but recurrent dreams are inevitably connected with some

sort of reincarnation remembrance. In the recurrent-dream phenomenon the dream is usually well remembered on awakening, to
the point that it is hard to shake even during the course of the day.
When it reoccurs it is usually identical to previous incidents; and in
some cases may advance the action, as it were, of the previous
dream, generally slightly but significantly.

It is the nature of dreams to be condensed versions of actual
occurrences. Consequently, we find that even ordinary dreams are
very short representations of what under ordinary logical conditions would be extended periods of time. In the recurrent dream
episodes the number of facts pertaining to a given situation are also
strongly condensed; that is to say, only the key words or facts are
flashed into the unconscious mind of the sleeper, much in the
nature of a telegram. On awakening, the key words are easily
remembered and can be written down, if necessary, in order to be
followed up. Recurrent dreams are generally very emotional and
frequently deal with situations involving death or tragedy or, at the
very least, highly dramatic conditions. It is also significant that the
dreamer always sees himself or herself in the dream not as an
outsider but as a participant. If the physical figure of the sleeper is
not actually perceived, a sense of presence is nevertheless felt.

In this respect recurrent dreams differ greatly from ordinary
psychic experiences, even those that may be ascribed to intervention from deceased individuals trying to communicate with the
sleeper and using the sleeper as a medium for their unexpressed
communications. This is an important point, since those not too
familiar with reincarnation research but otherwise cognizant of
ESP and psychic phenomena tend to substitue ordinary ESP communications for genuine reincarnation explanations. The difference
between a psychic experience where the sleeper merely acts as the
receiver of information from a deceased individual and those where
the sleeper is himself involved as a *principal* is very important: In
recurrent dreams containing reincarnation material, the sleeper
sees himself or feels himself in the scene. Where the sleeper merely acts as medium, he never puts himself into the scene but feels,
very probably, that he is only an observer, standing on the outside,
as it were, looking in.

The people to whom events of this kind happen come from all
walks of life, all social backgrounds, and all ages. There is nothing

specific about them, nothing that would single them out as being prone to reincarnation memories or even to psychic phenomena. Having ESP or experiencing something along psychic lines is in no way unnatural or supernatural, and people who partake of these experiences can be any kind of people—you and me included.

Diane Rogers is in her early forties, a Chicago housewife and mother who works as a film laboratory technician. Her husband is a supervisor for Swift, and she has two children, ages ten and fifteen. When she first contacted me, it was because reincarnation memories and other psychic experiences had disturbed her. She wanted to know what they meant and if necessary how to cope with them. Her interest in the occult was practically nonexistent at first, and she had only once before been hypnotized, three years prior to our meeting, when she wanted to stop smoking.

When we met at the Hampshire House in Chicago, she was visibly nervous. Her face was pale. She smoked one cigarette after another, since the attempt to stop smoking had evidently not been a success. "I have had numerous dreams and feelings and most of them involve my husband or close friends," she explained. "One dream involved my husband and another woman, and in it I actually saw them on the street in front of a restaurant in the town where I was then living, Harvey, Illinois. Her face was not clear, but on her sweater was the initial *J*. In the dream I was very upset, and I remember stamping on my husband's foot and kicking him in the shin and then walking away. A few days later I learned through a friend that my husband had indeed had an affair with a young lady whose initial was *J*. She worked in the restaurant I had seen in my dream. I confronted him with the evidence of the dream and he admitted it. But he wanted to know how I knew about it." Telling her husband that she had dreamed the information would not have done any good, so she simply told him that a friend had given her the information. Since Mrs. Rogers had expressed a desire to be regressed hypnotically in order to learn about any previous lives, I wondered whether she had ever had any indication that she had lived before.

"I've always had a strong interest in the pre-Civil War South," she explained. I read everything and anything I can get my hands on, and I am very interested in the period but only until the middle of the war, and then I don't seem to care any longer. Coming back from Florida in 1968 I was going through Georgia and admiring the countryside. My father-in-law was driving, and we were just passing through a wooded area. Suddenly I had a strong impulse to go down a certain side road, but I am sure if I had gone down that road I would have discovered something about a previous life in Georgia. I have a feeling that I lived as a slave."

"Have you ever had any specific dreams in which you saw yourself as someone else?" I inquired.

"I've seen myself wearing long dresses but I couldn't see the face, just the clothes. I've seen myself drowning. It is always dark in those dreams, and it seems to have something to do with a wooden bridge. I have a recurrent dream about being in the water and it being dark."

Karen Massey contacted me in New York because of what seemed to her a puzzling experience. Consequently, I met with her in October 1972 when I visited Houston, Texas. The attractive young woman had had some premonitory dreams most of her growing years. About five years ago, she began to feel that she really belonged in the France of about 1740. She kept seeing herself dressed in long fluffy dresses. In another scene she saw herself in what she considers the early eighteen-hundreds, somewhere in an area that had not been fully settled as yet. She and her husband were living in a little log cabin. She remembers that he had asked her to go out and get something from outside of the cabin near a ravine. When she went out, she saw an Indian standing beside a tree. Frightened, she yelled for her husband to come out. She remembers her husband telling her not to move, and then she saw him shoot the Indian in the stomach. It was a horrible dream but very real to her—she even felt the leaves crunching under her feet.

Although the conscious material was not overwhelming in terms of evidence, I decided to hypnotize her to see whether additional evidence might surface under hypnosis. Karen was fairly nervous but eventually calmed down sufficiently for me to be able to put her under. When I had reached 165 years prior to her birth, she reported seeing a little boy with red hair but did not know who he was. At minus 200 however she described a village and someone named Molly. Molly was a four-year-old girl she knew then, she explained in the hypnotic state. I took Karen, or Molly that is, back to age eighteen, and now there was also a boy named John Bradbury. The scene, according to the hypnotized subject, was England in the seventeen-hundreds, and the location was called Abanel. Karen now became someone else, even to her facial expressions. Under questioning she disclosed that her name was Barbara and that her father was dead and that her mother was named Margaret. She was fifteen when I "found" her, but I quickly advanced Barbara to age twenty-five and discovered that she had had several children in the meantime, being now married to the aforesaid John Bradbury. At age forty, Barbara was still alive but "very tired," a grandmother now. Eventually she "just lays down and dies."

"After she dies what happens to her?" I inquired of the hypnotized subject.

"She just watches things and everybody."

"Where does she go?"

"Into the air."

"Does she meet anyone there whom she knows?"

"Papa."

"How long does she stay up there?"

"Until somebody needs her."

"Does Barbara get born again?"

"She just keeps looking around from there, looking at things."

"What is she looking for?"

"Probably John and her children."

I suggested that the subject follow Barbara forward in time until she reached another incarnation. "Where is Barbara now?"

"She's me, her name is Karen Lamb but they call her Kay."

"Does she know she's Barbara?"

"She could if she wanted to."

"Was there anything Barbara didn't finish that Kay could finish?"

"No, but she just shouldn't be unhappy. She's unhappy not knowing if she'll ever see her kids again."

I then changed my line of questioning, asking the subject to describe Barbara more closely.

"She has pretty hair in curls, green eyes and they sparkle

when she smiles. Some women don't like her because of John Bradbury. He was Molly's boyfriend originally and he married Barbara. Molly married somebody else." Shortly afterward I brought Karen out of her hypnotic state. On awakening she remembered absolutely nothing of what she had said while hypnotized. "I don't remember any Molly" she said firmly.

Juanita Thomson is a housewife in California. When she was about ten years old she had a vivid dream that she never forgot. In this dream she was easily able to draw a picture of the vision. The road curved to the right and then led into town. There were hills on both sides, and in the center of the town there was a corner with a drugstore on it. In the dream, Mrs. Thomson had no idea why she was in that particular town, on that particular street. It reoccurred very vividly between ages sixteen and seventeen. In June 1961, when she was eighteen years old, she was married. A few months afterward her husband and she drove from Springfield, Missouri, to southern New Jersey. They took the northern route (Route 66) that led through parts of Ohio. When they neared the town of Zanesville, Mrs. Thomson seemed to feel that she had been there before; the road fit her dream experience. She did not make a point of it, and they did not stop. But as they drove through town, she was suddenly thinking, "There are a lot more houses now." Since this was a unique experience, Mrs. Thomson wondered what it meant. "I have no idea what this is all about since I have not been east of Missouri except as an infant when my father was stationed in South Carolina."

A good case in point where great contrasts are obvious is the case of Helen J. of Philadelphia, Pennsylvania. She has had a recurrent dream that was neither very long nor mysterious, except that it involved her being in a place unknown to her in her present existence. "The place is a big house with a large number of rooms. There is a part of it which I keep locked up and do not use. Although I live in this place, there seems to be some anxiety, unhappiness, and even fear. In each dream it is exactly the same place, the same feeling. I have never lived in such a place and could never afford the furniture, such expensive furniture as it had. I am not interested in finding out whether I was great in another life. I would like to know what the dream means. I am a Negro of modest means, and I consider myself intelligent, with some education."

Sally Sarnoskie is a housewife in Pennsylvania. She has had various psychic experiences all her life, mainly precognitions. But the most disturbing event in her life is a recurrent dream that used to occur to her many times as a child, all through high school. Eventually it faded away and has not come back to her since. To this day, she does not understand its true meaning.

The dream always started out in the same way. She saw herself as a small girl, running, full of terror, down a red brick road. She knew that this little girl was herself. As the girl looked behind her, she saw a man swinging a rope with a noose on the end. He was chasing her, and she ran and ran and finally came to a bush. The bush had no leaves at all. The little girl could see straight through it. She hid behind the bush and the man kept coming after her. When he came upon her and was ready to put the rope on her, Mrs. Sarnoskie would wake up. Was she reliving death at the hands of an evil person? Everytime this dream occurred to her, she found herself in a state of absolute terror upon awakening. It would be easier to dismiss this as merely a symbolic dream capable of the usual psychoanalytical interpretation were it not for the fact that all her other dreams were totally dissimilar to this one.

Mrs. Lois Smith of Arkansas is married and has five children, one of whom is deceased. Their eight-room house is in the country, and she leads an ordinary middle-class life. Yet, since age five or six, strange things have happened to her that seem to be beyond the reach of a five-year-old. She would say things that were out of context for her age and surroundings, which amazed her elders. Ever since then, she has developed precognition to a high degree, has been able to foretell future events, and has practiced extrasensory perception in many other forms. There are witnesses to every one of her predictions that have come true, but I am not concerned here with her psychic experiences as such.

There are two dreams she has had repeatedly. The first recurring dream concerns an event in which she sees herself alone in bed at night, and she then sees a man come in and stab her with a knife in the left side. At this precise moment she feels exactly where the knife goes in. It stings her and there is much pain after that, for she is dying. This dream has come to her many times.

Another dream is more detailed. In this she sees herself on a ship she describes as a clipper ship. Mrs. Smith has no knowledge of boats or ships, but the ship she sees in these recurring dreams seems to be of an earlier age. She remembers men wearing ruffles, and she remembers a number of children and turmoil. She has the feeling of a robbery and an exchange of riches for the lives of these children. One of the children reminds her of her own five-year-old daughter, Linda, but she's not sure of the resemblance. She sees the child playing under a blanket with her head covered. She describes the riches as being in brown or gray bags and very heavy. A passage on this ship is quite vivid in her memory. She describes it in great detail, even including the wooden paneling.

"The place seemed quite roomy and comfortable," she explains. "It was lit by some sort of light enclosed in a glass globe that hung on the walls here and there, but mostly it was dimly lit, which led me to believe it was nighttime. The color was amber, because it reflected off the wood of the ship. This gave the wood a soft, reddish color. At shoulder height there were strips of wood going around the boat's walls. The children," she explained, "were in another place on the same ship. This was located near a doorway. They seemed happy and contented and unafraid." She remembers having to stoop a little when entering through a curtain. She didn't feel frightened, and she remembered only being annoyed at having to be there at all. The strange thing was that she didn't feel as if she were participating in this event but rather that she was watching it, as if she were outside.

There were men coming into the ship from her left. An exchange was made, and the men were forming some kind of relay with the heavy sacks. They wore ruffles on their sleeves, while others were in odd clothing. She recalls thinking that they were peasants because of this and their very bad smell. They smelled of fish and oil. One of the men had a long knife stuck through his belt. The belt was like nothing she had ever seen before. It was more like a piece of material tied around the waist, and the knife was stuck through it. It was a curving knife with twine around the handle—very big, perhaps thirty inches long. It shone brightly, and she remembers being fascinated with the shine. She also recalls being repelled by the dirty appearance of the man who wore the belt and knife. He was bald, and the shine of his head was almost equal to that of the knife.

She recalls that the robbery was very quiet, and she had a feeling that the entire transaction had the cooperation of someone aboard the ship. Finally, she recalls that the men taking the heavy sacks upstairs were all wearing gray cloths wrapped around their heads—not Turkish style but so that they had a bald look at the top of their heads.

Now, Mrs. Smith has had no interest in pirate stories or ships or anything pertaining to the events depicted in her recurrent dreams. The vivid impression left each time she dreamt this—and she dreamt it many times in exactly the same fashion—did not fade as time went on. She got to wondering what it all meant. Eventually, she read books dealing with extrasensory perception, and eventually also she thought that it might indicate some kind of reincarnation memory. Only then did she decide to read books dealing with the subject of reincarnation, and she has since then read several. But at the time when the dreams occurred to her, there was no knowledge of the field or what it might mean to her.

✳

CHAPTER SEVEN

Déjà Vu Experiences as Possible Evidence for Reincarnation

ALMOST EVERYBODY has at one time or another had a sudden short experience called déjà vu—a distinct feeling that one has done something before, has been to a place before, or heard something said before that is now being enacted. Logical thinking tells one that this cannot be so because the event is just taking place, but there is a very strong feeling nevertheless that the scene one is just experiencing has been experienced before. This is generally followed by a nagging doubt as to whether one is correct about the situation, at the same time that there is a certainty that one is familiar with what is being said or done at that precise moment. Orthodox psychologists and psychiatrists have long explained this as a trick of memory. They say that people sometimes open a "false memory door" and thus experience a feeling of previous knowledge when in fact there is no such knowledge. But the same psychiatrists fail to tell us how the mind accomplishes this marvelous trick of "false memory doors." In this case, the commonly heard explanation for déjà vu is simply not sufficient. *Déjà vu* means "already seen" in French, but it covers experiences of "already heard" and "already known" as well. Foreknowledge without a logical base might be a better way of describing this phenomenon.

Hardly anyone goes through life without having at least one or more such experiences. They are probably among the most common forms of ESP phenomena. Undoubtedly, the majority of these déjà vu experiences can be explained on the basis of precognition. An experience is foreseen and not noted at the time. Later, when the experience becomes objective reality and one goes through it, one suddenly remembers "as if in a flash" that one has had knowledge of this particular experience before. In other words, the majority of déjà vu experiences are nothing more than forgotten precognitive incidents. However, there is a residue of such experiences that cannot be explained on this basis. Among them are such cases as people coming to a town or a house for the first time and having exact foreknowledge of what the house or town looks like—even to the point of knowing specific rooms, furniture, and arrangements in rooms and other details that are far beyond the scope of ordinary precognition. There is a thin line where the precognitive experience must end; precognitive experiences do not contain exhaustive details, including names, dates, arrangements in rooms, and so on, to the point where the details are so specific and so numerous that only a person who would have been familiar with the arrangements could have remembered them. In general, precognitive experiences are partial and stress certain salient points, a few details perhaps, but never the entire picture. When the number of remembered details becomes very large, we must always suspect reincarnation memories.

A young man in upstate New York went to a house he had never been to before in his lifetime. Upon arrival he became very excited and suddenly remembered every detail about the house he was about to enter. When he reached the upper story, he told his companions what lay around the corner and what the room to which they would next come would look like. All this was confirmed. Had this merely been a precognitive experience, he would have had a flash of himself coming to this house and might see himself enter it, but the foreknowledge of details would have been absent.

It would be erroneous to assume that all such déjà vu experiences have deeper significance or that they even represent important memories. Quite the opposite is true; the majority of such remembrances seem to be everyday details of no particular significance. They are, however, important in an indirect way; by heaping a number of commonplace memories one upon the other, a continual basis for remembering is established. As with all other psychic experiences, there is always an emotional base present. Purely logical or mechanical details are never remembered.

Mary Chappel is the youngest of four children of a dairyman. She lived in Missouri for twelve years before moving to California. Now thirty-eight years old and married, she has six children— three boys and three girls—and lives in a small town in the San Francisco Bay area. Mrs. Chappel has had various ESP experiences throughout most of her adult life. On June 9, 1970, she and her daughter Linda Gail were on a shopping expedition to the nearby town of Vallejo. Somehow she felt the urge to go back home by way of Sonoma, where there are a number of historical landmarks. They decided to stop at the old San Francisco Solarno Mission and tour it, especially General Vallejo's home. They followed the directions leading there:

"The oddest feeling came over us as soon as we got out of the car," Mrs. Chappel explained, "A feeling that we had been there before, but of course neither of us ever had. As we walked through the gardens and the house we could sense someone right at our shoulders, but no one was to be seen. It wasn't a scary feeling but a warm feeling, as if someone were saying, 'Welcome back, where have you been?'" Mrs. Chappel then continues her account: "The objects in the room seemed familiar, especially a piano in the living room and one of the upstairs bedrooms. It was all we could do to drag ourselves away, but we felt a pull back for months. Finally, we were able to go back on October 18, 1971. The feelings were stronger than ever, in fact, we even had tears in our eyes, tears of joy at being there again.

"While on this same trip we stopped at the Petaluma Adobe near Santa Rosa, another place that had belonged to General Vallejo. The same feeling of being home hit us, and we knew what was in some of the rooms before looking in at the doors. While walking on the upstairs balcony, the years seemed to melt away, and we could sense how things had been a hundred years before. Also, throughout the hour we were there we could smell flowers in bloom, although it was mid-October and there were no flowers around." Salvador Vallejo was a young officer in the Mexican Army serving in California. In 1833 he was sent to inspect Russian activities at Fort Ross near Bodega Bay. Eventually, the region became part of the United States, with the blessing and the advice of General Vallejo.

The curious thing about these short flashes from another existence is that they occur not only to people who may have an understanding of such previous situations, but also frequently to people to whom such earlier existences would be totally alien. When the information from a possible previous existence contains cultural, social, or historical information not available to the person in the present, the evidential value of the observation is of course that much greater. Naturally, there are just as many cases where an individual experiences a reincarnation flash from a lifetime in similar surroundings to his present ones.

Mrs. Helen Frank of Macon, Georgia, is a housewife. Her husband is a well-to-do businessman, she has two grown sons, and in her spare time she is the literary editor of *The Macon News*. She has always been interested in ESP, because she found that she possesses this power herself. On a number of occasions she would know about events that were happening at a distance, and she has a very close telepathic relationship with both her children. But the experience that shook her up most happened in the summer of 1966 when she and her husband were in Europe, traveling through Italy. They were leaving the Trevi Fountain in Rome during a light rain, crossing a narrow street, and hastening toward their waiting bus. Her husband was pulling her along, holding her by the hand so she wouldn't slip on the wet sidewalk. Suddenly, she happened to gaze fleetingly at one of several small enclosed gardens. Peeking through one of the wrought-iron doors, she saw a place that she instantly knew that she knew well, though she had never seen it before. "I felt as though I were home. I knew that if I cast my eyes around to the right I would see a statue of a mother and child. If I looked to the left, there would be an old tree with a bench around it. It did, and *they were there just as I knew they would be*."

But her husband was hurrying her back to the bus, so she could not stop and go in, though she wanted to very much. As he pulled her away, she recognized even the doorway of the house. Unfortunately, they could not go back because they left early the following morning. When she explained her startling experience to a friend, the friend kiddingly called her "another Bridey Murphy." Until then Helen Frank had never heard of Bridey Murphy, but eventually she caught up with the book and understood the reference. That was all she could consciously remember. Nothing like it ever occurred to her again nor had anything like it happened to her before the incident in Rome. Under the circumstances, I suggested regression through hypnosis, and on my next visit to Atlanta, Georgia, we met for that purpose. That was on November 8, 1968, and after some initial conversation we went over the matter of the courtyard in Rome once again.

"All the houses were enclosed with high fences," she explained. "You could see through a gate into the yard, and I was glancing at them as we went by. Suddenly I recognized the lintel over the door, that is the top part. I glanced at it and it looked very familiar. So I stopped, and although my husband was pulling me and said, 'Come on,' I said, 'Wait just a minute,' and I stopped completely at the gateway and looked in and I recognized the whole yard. I didn't look at the house; somehow or other it didn't occur to me to look at the house, but the doorway in the yard I recognized immediately. I knew I had been there. I knew that there would be the statue and over to the left an old tree with a bench of some sort around it and *I knew that I used to sit on it.* I looked for it and there it was."

"Did you see yourself in the picture?" I asked.

"I guess so," she replied, "but it was that courtyard that attracted me most strongly."

An excellent case in point, and perhaps a typical déjà vu experience, involves a young man from upstate New York by the name of Del Cook, who was a senior in high school, going on to college. Here is Mr. Cook's report:

In the spring of 1965 several friends of mine, Joseph D., Christy D., Peter P., Margaret P., Joanne B., and myself, Del Cook, were on our way to a Christian camp at Beaver Falls, New York, accompanied by Father George K., our group supervisor. We were going to visit this camp to inquire about spending two weeks there. Upon arriving, it occurred to me that the main building, which was four stories high, was familiar to me, but at that time we went to see the director of the camp so I ignored the impression. After meeting the director, we went to look around the area. Then the feeling that I had been there before began to increase, but I didn't tell the others. We went to the side of the large building. There was a pool there, but it was relatively new, and I didn't recognize it.

As time went on I felt more and more that I had been there before, even though I had never been in the area. I told the others to follow me around to the back of the house. Just before going into the door I realized it was the door to the kitchen. We went through the kitchen, but it was not very familiar. At this time I didn't think much about it being un-usual that I recognized the area. Then we went through the dining room to the stairs, and I told the others that I had seen the place before, even though I had never been there. I told them that I would show them around, so they agreed, but were a bit hesitant. Next I showed them the second and third floors, recognizing the rooms as we went. While on the third floor I told them that I would then show them the next floor. They asked where it was, as no stairs were apparent. I told them that the door to one side was the one that led up to the attic. They asked how I knew, and I told them that I remem-bered it from somewhere. We opened the door and there were the stairs. We went halfway up, and I told them that as they went through the door at the top of the stairs they would see some old pictures, and to the left there would be two trunks placed end to end. The first one had china, and the second had clothes in it. Then we went up the rest of the way, and the room was just as I described. The trunks were there containing the china and the clothes. All of this was out of the line of sight of where we were on the stairs when I told them there was a door at the top of the stairs as well. Then we went through a bit more of the house and went out. Outside I saw a dog, a Russian wolfhound, and I remembered its name. I can't remember the name now, though. It began barking, and a lady came out of the house and called it by the name to stop barking. At this time I was fourteen years old.

Sometimes the line between prevision or clairvoyance and later verification in objective reality is very thin, and the memory of the earlier impression is not entirely erased or suppressed. There is, then, a vague or uncertain feeling of having heard someone say something or having seen something or someone before, and when the event actually takes place, one realizes that this has not really happened until this very moment. A good case of this kind occurred to a colleague and friend of the previous communicator. John Leadley was also a senior in an upstate New York high school and would later attend the University of Notre Dame. Here is his report:

> Del Cook and I were in English workshop on May 15, 1969. For several days previous to this particular afternoon, I had been thinking that something Del had said to me was very unusual. This thing that he had said was, "Did you know that gluttony was a moral affection?" I didn't give this too much thought during these days, except that it was such an unusual thing for him to say. Also, I had a mental picture of him turning to a certain page in the book and then saying that. Then on the fifteenth I was sitting at a desk in the English room, when it seemed as though I had seen the whole scene, with the people in exactly those positions, before. Then Del said, "Did you know that gluttony was a moral affection?"

Now, a phrase of such unusual connotation is certainly not explicable on the basis of coincidence—if there is, indeed, such a thing as coincidence. Here we have a similar experience to déjà vu, except that it is the reverse—the confirmation follows the impression that it has already happened.

Ilsa Brown is a librarian in Mansfield, Ohio. All her life she has been having psychic experiences. When she went to boarding school in her native Germany, in Dresden, she went to the so-called English garden, where she had never been before. Immediately upon arriving at the garden, she knew her way around and knew that she had been there before; yet, she was unable to pinpoint the time or occasion. Since then she has had many experiences in which she would arrive at a town or place only to recognize the place as something she had seen before. In her case, certain smells seem to evoke certain memories. In other cases, it is sound or a pictorial impression that seem to stimulate the faculty of recalling an earlier impression.

Betty Fiocco, of Los Angeles, is a housewife with many years of psychic experiences. She has now read a great deal on ESP and other forms of psychic consciousness, but in previous years when the bulk of her experiences took place, she had no knowledge of parapsychology and was stumped by the things that happened to her. Of interest here is an incident that occurred to her in a German restaurant in La Jolla, California. The restaurant had been open only a few years when Betty Fiocco and her husband paid it a visit. Upon seeing the German owner of the place, whose name is Ernie, she instantly felt that she had known him before, and he felt the same way about her. Now, to be sure, this did not have a romantic connotation at all. They glanced at each other casually, and they knew each other. This went on for the several visits that the Fioccos paid the restaurant afterward. The entire thing troubled her so much that she tried time and again to figure out where she had met him. At the same time, he was trying to figure out where he had met the strange lady before. Finally, she had enough nerve to go over to him and ask, "Where have I ever met you before?" and it developed that they had, indeed, never met. He had come from Europe recently and gone on to Chicago and from there to his present place.

During World War II, a soldier found himself in Belgium. While his buddies were wondering how to enter a certain house in a particular small town in Belgium, he showed them the way in and went ahead of them up the stairs, explaining as he went up where each room was. When he was questioned after this about having been there before, he denied ever having left his home in America, and he spoke the truth. He could not explain how he had suddenly found himself possessed of knowledge he did not have in his normal condition.

✳

CHAPTER EIGHT

How to Prove
Previous Lives

IN CASES INVOLVING REINCARNATION, an author should not rest with the presentation of the story alone but should verify at least a substantial amount of the material obtained, either in flashes of conscious knowledge or through hypnosis. When the story is presented without the proper verification, it becomes nothing more than an interesting account. Such, in my opinion, is the case with much of the material to be found in *Here and Hereafter,* by Ruth Montgomery.

A different slant is taken by Joan Grant's account of her research, especially when it involves ancient Egypt. Here we must consider Miss Grant's own involvement with Egyptian archeology and the possibility that the material rose from her own unconscious mind. But if this were not so, the need to verify some of the material involving Egyptian archeology is very great and, in my opinion, entirely capable of producing information, data, and details that could be considered genuine only if they were indeed stemming from the communicator or from the previous incarnation claimed. Surely in delving into the mystery of a previous lifetime one is allowed to ask certain test questions in order to establish identity beyond a shadow of a doubt. If such questions are not asked and the proper research not undertaken, then the case becomes weak and, while it may be genuine, lacks the necessary convincing elements.

The cases I am presenting in this chapter are not lacking in research where research was possible, but are incomplete in other ways. Either there is not enough material available on the case in point or the material is of a kind that rings true but cannot be verified, no matter how much one would like, due to lack of research sources or to other technical reasons. Even though in these cases I was unable to present a completely convincing picture, all the cases here discussed are incapable of alternative explanations and therefore fit in with the concept of reincarnation memories as I have established it earlier. In some cases, additional sessions with the person involved might have yielded additional results, but this was not always possible. Reincarnation is not a matter of life or death to the one to whom the memories occur, and a researcher such as I may not always be free to travel to distant cities to follow up on each case, much as he would like.

I am presenting these partial or fractional cases here to show how common among all of us is the fleeting glimpse into a previous lifetime. That it is not a freak experience that happens to a few but is indeed far more common than is realized by most researchers, let alone the ordinary man in the street.

Whenever people have flashes of memories pertaining to earlier lives, these flashes are generally brief and are often confused and out of context. It is sometimes years before these people realize that what appear to them as either waking visions or strong dreams are actually part of an earlier lifetime. Frequently, the puzzle doesn't seem to work out and the pieces do not fall into place, but occasionally people do realize that what appear to them in this form has some meaning and are not merely figments of their imagination or just another dream.

In a number of cases there seems to be a relationship between psychic ability and reincarnation memories, although this does not mean that only those who have ESP have reincarnation flashes or that those who have reincarnation flashes are also psychic, but there are a number of cases in which both abilities coexist.

Rosemary Benoit is a twenty-eight-year-old housewife in Massachusetts. She remembers far back, even as far back as when she was only one year old. Today she wonders whether she has lived before. Often she would sit knitting a sweater, which is a job needing some concentration, when suddenly there would be a quick flash, and before her eyes, before her mind's eyes, she would see a vision of two girls coming home from school and a driveway of a house—a house she had never seen before except in these visions. All of a sudden she would remember this as if it were a dream from long ago. She didn't know where this place was, but she knew that she had been there.

What she saw involved a black car parked on a hill. A man was in the driver's seat, a man she instinctively knew to be her father. She hugged him, and it was nighttime. The car was standing on a dirt road. There was a large pine tree just next to where the car was parked and a log cabin below. They were waiting for someone. Her father wasn't the father she has in this lifetime. He was a strange man, and yet she knew he was her father. She, herself, was in the back seat as her father got out of the car. Next she saw herself out of the car also, playing with the bark of a tree—peeling it. Then someone called to her, and she ran down the hill behind some older children. The name Edwina flashed through her mind. Consciously, she does not know this name, yet in the vision she felt she had been there—that she was young, and that it was she who ran down that hill. She clearly saw this girl running last among the children—a girl with long hair, in a plain dress with a ruffled hem and a ruffled bodice. The hem was just above the ankle, the dress had some red and white on it, and she also wore long white stockings.

She began to wonder, Who was Edwina? The name sounded strange to her. Of course, she felt that perhaps this was something from her own childhood memory. She thought about it consciously, and she asked questions of her relatives. The name Edwina did not occur in her family. No such scene had ever taken place in her own lifetime, and yet she is possessed of an extraordinary memory going back to age one.

When I questioned her about details of this vision, she recalled that the car was one of those that were in style perhaps in the 1920s or early 1930s. She remembers seeing similar cars in old movies or on television, especially those dealing with Al Capone and his days. The windshield had a bar in the center; the interior was brown, perhaps leather or suede. Beyond that, she cannot recall any details, but there is a haunting feeling that she was Edwina running down a hill in another lifetime.

Ouija boards are the least likely tools to obtain verifiable information in psychic research, as I have often pointed out, and yet, once in awhile a Ouija board can be useful in research. Now, a Ouija board is nothing more than a piece of wood inscribed with the letters of the alphabet, numerals, and a few simple words like *yes, no,* and *maybe.* Upon it is placed a wooden contraption called the indicator, usually very lightweight, sometimes made of glass instead of wood. Upon this indicator rest the hands of two or more people participating in the experiment. These hands must be applied lightly. Naturally, the movements of the indicator across the board are not due to any spirit action per se but are due to the muscular action of the hands, or rather the *persons* whose hands are placed upon the indicator. But the motivation in moving the indicator to certain letters and thus spelling words and sentences may be due to another control than that of the person operating the board.

I have already pointed out in many of my books that I do not advise the use of Ouija boards by the average person because it presents certain dangers to those who have deep trance mediumship and are not aware of it at the time they first use such a board. But I do feel that occasionally this board may be an instrument for tapping the unconscious in a verifiable manner.

A strange case in point is the case of Mr. and Mrs. Atta, who live in Columbus, Ohio. Fascinated with extrasensory perception for some time, the couple had acquired a Ouija board and were trying to communicate through it with certain deceased entities. Having considered it merely a toy at first, the Attas took their board somewhat more seriously when it started to give them information pertaining to the husband.

It all started one evening in 1968 when they had used the board to amuse some of their guests. After the guests had left, Mrs. Atta and her husband sat down alone and tried the board again. This time the communicator, whoever it was, had immediate reference to the husband. The communicator in this case was a woman named Rochelle, who claimed to have been the wife of Mrs. Atta's husband in a previous incarnation. "Did you know Pete in his lifetime?" Mrs. Atta asked. The board indicated assent. "How long ago?" "One hundred and five years ago," said the board without a moment's hesitation. Stimulated by this exchange, Mrs. Atta then pursued the question. It developed that her husband, Pete, had been known as Robert Hinis, and that he had lived during the Civil War. Rochelle claimed to have been his wife at that time. At the time of his death, the board explained, Mr. Hinis had been twenty-five years old.

"Where was your home?" asked Mrs. Atta.

"Blacksburg, Virginia," came the answer.

"Where was Rob born?"

"Patascala, Virginia."

"Where were you born?"

"Blacksburg."

"What year was Rob born?"

"Thirty-eight."

"What year were you born?"

"Thirty-eight."

"How old were you when you died?"

"Twenty-four."

Mrs. Atta stopped the board and did a quick bit of arithmetic. If Rob had been born in 1838 and died at the age of twenty-five, he had died in the year 1863. Now, Rochelle said she had known him a hundred and five years ago, which also gets us back to 1863. The Civil War lasted from 1861 to 1865. It would be very difficult to do such quick arithmetic without time to think. Besides this, Mrs. Atta knew that her husband was not making this up or trying to play a practical joke on her, and as far as she was concerned, she certainly had no knowledge of either the character of Robert Hinis nor of the dates mentioned by his alleged wife, Rochelle. She questioned the communicator further.

How had her husband died? It turned out that he had been shot. He had been a scout and a colonel at the same time. This threw Mrs. Atta off, for she could not conceive of a scout being a colonel also. However, there were scout regiments in the Civil War with all the necessary ranks among their officers. A scout, in terms of Civil War history, does not mean a Boy Scout but simply a regiment of advance troops.

It developed further that Rochelle and her children had all died together in a fire, and that this fire had been due to war action. Pete, as Rob in his previous lifetime, had killed many men in defense of the United States government. The Confederate soldiers had burned down their house. Somehow the attachment Rochelle had had for her husband, Robert, in the nineteenth century had carried over to his new incarnation as Pete, and she felt she still should help him and his new wife get on as best they could.

After the sessions with the Ouija board, Mrs. Atta felt sort of foolish about the whole thing. She really did not believe that the communication was genuine, but to assure herself that there was nothing to it and to end the matter once and for all, she did write some letters about the period and people involved to what she considered the proper sources of information. These included the Attorney General's department in Roanoke, Virginia; the General Services Administration at the National Archives in Washington, D.C.; the Clerk of the County Court House of Montgomery County in Christianburg, Virginia; and the Clerk and Treasurer at Blacksburgh, Virginia, a Mrs. Rochelle Brown. She managed to find that there was, indeed, a Blacksburg, Virginia, in existence, although she could not locate Patascala, Virginia. However, she found there was a Palasky near Blacksburg and wondered if the communicator on the Ouija board had misspelled the word, as she had misspelled many other words. This, Mrs. Atta soon found out, is par for the course when you deal with a Ouija board. Strangely, she could not get anything else out of the communicator, who had called herself Rochelle, beyond this material; at any rate, nothing that proved to be of much value.

When replies came to her inquiries, she felt differently about the matter, however. There was a Robert Hinis from Christianburg County, Virginia, who had died in the Civil War at about the time the Robert Hinis whom the communicator, Rochelle, had spoken of had died.

One might go through life without ever remembering anything from an alleged previous lifetime until something starts one to thinking. Frequently, these are parallels to what one might have experienced in a previous incarnation, and it is the similarity between the two events or places that causes the recall.

Mrs. Betty James is a horse breeder in Pennsylvania. She is in her late thirties, the mother of two lovely daughters, and college-educated. Her interests in life are varied. In addition to caring for her family, she does volunteer work for the Red Cross, works with the handicapped in nursing homes, and is generally active in the community.

Early in her childhood she had frequently had the feeling that something, or rather someone, was missing in her life. Although she was happy with her parents and her many friends, the feeling persisted. She often felt out of place among her family and friends, somehow vaguely searching for someone who wasn't there.

Some friends of hers were having difficulty in caring for their aged father. Since her oldest girl was in college, she decided to spend two days each week with them in order to care for this elderly gentleman until he passed away. For some strange reason she could not understand, there was a change in her attitude toward her own family. Whenever she left in the evening to come home to her own family, whom she dearly loves, she felt as if she were leaving her true home to spend the night and the remainder of the week with strangers. Every day when she returned to the home of the aged man for whom she was now caring, she felt as if she were coming home to her own house. As soon as she crossed the threshold of this man's house, she felt complete—like a whole person. No longer did she have the feeling that someone was absent, but a sense of peace and serenity came over her just as soon as she entered the old man's house.

What confused the matter was the fact that she had several dreams while sleeping in the house. In one of them, the deceased wife of the old man took her on a tour of her home in another town. Afterward, she asked his children whether the descriptions she had of their mother and their childhood residence were correct. To her amazement she was informed that they were.

In another dream, she saw this woman whom she had never met in life; and when her son showed her a picture of this same woman, she almost fainted, for it was the woman she had seen in her dreams. Could it be, then, that this old gentleman, so near death, was thinking of his earlier life and in some way his thoughts had become transferred to her? she argued. But this would not explain the reason for the deep sense of fulfillment she had every time she set foot into his house.

Life has been good to Mrs. James in many ways. She has been

happy all her life, and yet the peace and the feeling of having come home that she experienced when going to the old man's house was something beyond her comprehension. After the period of caring for the old man had ended, she felt more miserable and discontented than she had ever been in her life. Returning to her own home, she had lost that precious sense of fulfillment and contentment she had had for a short time in someone else's home. Mrs. James cannot help feeling that she knew this man in a previous lifetime and that, perhaps, she was discharging some form of karma.

Ellen was born in New York City. When she was ten years old, she became aware of another young girl, who appeared to her in visions and daydreams. Somehow she knew that the young girl used to be herself, even though she did not look like Ellen. A certain scene kept impressing itself upon her mind over and over. In this scene, the young girl was riding a horse, and the horse jumped a hurdle and fell, and when the girl fell off the horse, she died.

She saw very clearly how the little girl was dressed. She wore a red jacket and riding pants. There were large tracts of land around, and she had the feeling that this was somewhere in the United States. She also felt that this was in an earlier century, and at one point she got the feeling that it was around 1881. The girl had dark hair and didn't look like the present Ellen at all. There were other scenes: She would see this girl in a kind of library wearing a long dress—a dress going down to the ankles—and the library was lit by big white bubbling lights. By bubbling lights Ellen described clusters of what she thought were bulblike crystal containers. She wasn't sure whether they were gaslights or electric lights. In this scene the girl was reading a book. The book was open in her hands, and then the scene just faded out. Somehow Ellen felt very emotional about this other girl. Somehow she felt she liked her and felt sorry for her. She had a strong feeling of emotional attachment for this other girl—a feeling as if she knew her.

Over the years these two scenes stayed with her. The last time she had experienced these daydreams was only a few months before she met me. Then, a few weeks before she came to seek my help, she had a terrifying experience. She woke up in the middle of the night, sat bolt upright in bed, and started talking, and yet she felt as if it wasn't she talking at all but some other person speaking through her. All the time, she heard every word she was saying, unable to control what came out of her mouth. By this time, she was fully awake and realized what she had said. What she had spoken was one sentence: "Clara J. Wiston, Clara J. Wiston is coming for me."

She was surprised at herself. She had never heard that name before. What did it mean? Who was Clara Wiston? At that moment she was fully awake and thought it was all nonsense and foolishness. For awhile she entertained the notion of looking up whether there was indeed a Clara Wiston somewhere, but she really didn't know where to begin to look, so she dropped it, and the matter was of no further interest to her. Then she read one of my books and decided to question me about it. When she came to see me, we went over the entire incident carefully.

It developed that she wasn't sure of the girl's age. Perhaps she saw her at various times of her life; that is to say, first as a child of ten and then later as an adolescent. I sent her home with the request to try to return, as it were, in her daydreaming or even in the nocturnal dream state to the period in which Clara Wiston lived and to try to get additional information. On the night of July 3, 1967, she started to work on herself. "Who is Clara Wiston and where was she born?"

That night she had a dream, and although she could not remember all its details, she was able to write down quite a bit on awakening. In her dream, the girl was talking socially to a gathering of people and kept mentioning two places—Cresskill or Crestmont and another place called Crow something (she couldn't quite get the word that followed Crow). Subsequently, research in local libraries yielded some results.

There isn't a Cresskill or Crestmont anywhere in New York State, including Long Island, but there is a Crown Point, which dates back to 1755. It is located near Ticonderoga, on the neck of land connecting Lake George and Lake Champlain. During the Revolutionary War this was a location of some importance, as it fell to the American troops in 1775. Of course, the place might also have been Croton-on-Hudson or any name beginning with a syllable like Crow.

What interested me more was the name Clara Wiston. Wiston seemed to me a very uncommon name, and so it turned out to be. My own research in genealogical sources confirmed my suspicion that the name Wiston was indeed a rare name, but finally I discovered in a book called *The Pioneers of Massachusetts*, by Charles H. Pope, published in Boston in 1900, that a Wiston family did indeed exist in New England as early as 1665. John Wiston, father of Joseph Wiston, lived in Scituate, Massachusetts, in that year. Evidently the name is of New England origin, for I also discovered in *Massachusetts Soldiers and Sailors of the Revolutionary War*, Boston, 1908, on page 660, that one Edmond Wiston lived in 1778, a Joseph Wiston in 1778, and a Simon Wiston in 1776. Was Clara Wiston a descendant of that New England family?

Mildred Corkran grew up in Whittier, California. The Corkrans—Mildred, both parents, a brother, and a sister—came from Ohio in 1901 and settled in southern California. Mildred was born in that state. She says she was a lonely child despite her brother and sister—always playing alone or being with animals. She married for the first time at age eighteen and had three children—two boys and a girl—but her husband passed on in 1931. Later she married again, but that marriage did not work out, and she has been divorced for the past twelve years. Her husband held the rank of major in the Air Force.

Of average height, she has dark brown hair and sparkling blue eyes. She is far livelier than her years would suggest, but all in all, is a typical upper-middle-class lady with average interests.

The event that amazed, if it didn't upset, Mrs. Corkran happened in July 1956. At that time she was living in Modesto. That afternoon Mrs. Corkran decided to go shopping to Stockton, which is about thirty miles away. She asked a friend by the name of Greta Boytel to come along for the ride. Her friend readily agreed. To make the shopping expedition more interesting, she asked her friend whether she had ever seen the University of the Pacific. Her friend said she hadn't, so they decided to drive past it to look at it.

It was just about four o'clock in the afternoon, and the two ladies were talking of nothing in particular and laughing, "for we were both in a very relaxed mood. Shopping does bring out the best in women sometimes." They were winding their way through the afternoon traffic when all of a sudden Mrs. Corkran felt very strange.

"I had the oddest feeling, as if something had washed over me," she said.

All of a sudden she was no longer on the road, driving her car through the city of Stockton. Instead, she seemed to be in a different place. She saw a path in front of her, flanked on both sides by several large white old-fashioned houses with trees. The houses were two stories high and were set back from the street a little bit with picket fences, and there were no sidewalks in front of them—only a kind of dirt path and rows of trees on what she knew was the parkway.

Suddenly, she noticed a woman walking up the pathway, with her back toward her so that she could not observe the woman's face. The woman then stepped to the left and walked off the side of the road. At this instant, Mrs. Corkran knew that this woman was she *herself*. Although she did not know the age or period this woman lived in, she seemed grown up.

Then, ahead of that alter ego of hers, Mrs. Corkran noticed a fence and a small hill. The woman kept walking toward that hill with a picket fence around it, and then the whole vision vanished. Mrs. Corkran found herself back in her driver's seat. The car was still running through traffic, and she felt rather strange, as if she had just been deflated.

"Is there anything wrong with you?" her friend asked, worry in her voice. Apparently, Mrs. Corkran had suddenly become very quiet and looked odd. Her friend thought she had been taken ill. The odd feeling stayed with Mrs. Corkran for about an hour, and then it slowly went away. Yet the impression was so vivid she could never forget it. She thought about it many times, realizing full well that she had never been to this place in her life. To her it did not look like California but some place "back East." Although the incident felt as if it had taken a long time, it was actually only a second or two. She had never lost control of the car.

I questioned Mrs. Corkran about the appearance of the woman she had seen in her vision. "She had on a light skirt, and it was down to here," she said, indicating her ankles, "and either a jacket or loose top, but that is about all I can remember." She is equally sure that the houses she saw were not of a kind that have ever been built in California, but reminded her of houses in the eastern part of the United States. No further visions of this kind ever occurred to her.

Mild incidents involving ESP, such as knowing who might be calling before the telephone rings or a feeling that a dead relative was present in what used to be his house contributed somewhat to her understanding, if not acceptance, of psychic phenomena. The only other incident tying in with her amazing experience in Stockton happened in the summer of 1967.

Not far from her present home is the old capital of California—Columbia. One afternoon she decided to take a ride up there with her dog. She had been there before many times, and she had a feeling of belonging there. This time it was particularly strong.

Columbia is a small gold-mining town that the state has turned into a national park. Mrs. Corkran was walking along the main street and looking at the restored buildings when all of a sudden it seemed to her as if there weren't any buildings there at all, and again she saw a woman walking ahead of her. The woman was the same person she had seen before in traffic at Stockton, when her first vision overcame her, but this time she wore different clothes. The old-fashioned clothes this woman was wearing were not the kind the people in Columbia put on for tourists. The woman walking ahead of her wore dark gray clothes, a big bonnet, and some very high, heavy shoes, but, even more interesting, she seemed to be floating ahead of her rather than walking on the ground. All at once Mrs. Corkran realized it was she who was walking ahead of her in the road, and that she saw a vision of something that had happened in the past—*her* past.

Again the woman did not turn around so she could not see her face, but the certainty that she was looking at an earlier incarnation of herself remained with her. The feeling did not leave her for several hours. Although Mrs. Corkran was sure that she herself was the woman she had seen, there was no physical resemblance between the apparition and her present appearance. But as she grows older, a vague and yet persistent feeling comes back to her again and again. She sees in her mind's eye trees, a stream, a quiet place somewhere in the country, and she knows at the same time that she has been there. Every day she yearns more for it, wishing she could be there again.

CHAPTER NINE

Reincarnation Memories in Children

IT IS NOT UNCOMMON for a young child to speak of places, situations, and people that a child couldn't possibly have known. Those unfamiliar with the record of reincarnation research are quick to attribute all such unusual utterances to childish fantasies. But what is one to make of entire sentences formed by a two- or three-year-old child, using words the child could not possibly have heard or absorbed even if they had been spoken in his immediate family? What is one to make of complicated, even sophisticated, descriptions of places from the historical past in households where history is not a household word? The number of cases where small children, even as little as one year old, speak in coherent and intelligent fashion of places and people they could not possibly know, apart from the fact that they could not possibly speak in such a fashion anyway, is impressive. Some of these cases have been called "miracle children," or *Wunderkinder*. With very rare exceptions, however, they are not miracle children but children who happen to remember something from their earlier lives. Even those few who are genuine miracle children are very likely to be in that position not due to some special talent within themselves but because of what they have brought into this life from another one.

In the majority of cases that have come to my attention, the ability to recall seeming bits and pieces from an earlier lifetime gradually fades out toward the time when the child goes to school.

In some cases the memory returns around the ages of seventeen or eighteen, and then usually with a vengeance and in greater detail. But at that point the rational capacity of the person as well as some educational background must be taken into account when evaluating the evidence. With a little child below the age of five, such problems are of less impact. On the average, a child begins to speak in coherent sentences after age two, in many cases only when reaching age three. The ability to describe places and situations outside the immediate family does not usually begin until age four or five. Even if one takes a certain amount of fantasy into account, and many children refer to invisible friends as part of their development, there remains a hard core of evidential cases where all these explanations must be ruled out.

"Had I not been familiar with the theory of reincarnation, I would have ignored Amy-Kay," states Diane Lebo of Indiana. The unusual incident she was reporting to me concerned her two-year-old daughter by that name. The family had spent the day with friends out of town; the little girl had missed her afternoon nap and her mother knew that she would soon be asleep on the ride home. As they were riding, the mother noticed the little girl swaying from side to side in her seat and slowly getting a certain look in her eyes that came just before the child fell asleep. They were passing a familiar road now, and Mrs. Lebo said, casually, "There is the road to Nonnie's house." The word "road" somehow must have jogged the little girl's memory. Suddenly she started to mumble: "He killed me . . . that man killed me . . . that man killed me *in the road* . . . he killed me . . . I was born in the road and that man killed me, he stomped on me . . ."

After this outburst, and ignoring her mother's questions, the child went back to sleep.

For a two-year-old child, such expressions seem out of place. Mrs. Lebo also noted that the child had been using strange words ever since she began to talk. For instance, instead of saying "blanket," she would say "cover." On one occasion at the dinner table, she informed the family, "I picked cotton . . . I and Mommy." Mrs. Lebo quite rightly points out that a two-year-old simply doesn't know words like born and stomped, let alone cotton.

Mrs. Raymond Killela, who lives in Indiana, contacted me to

tell me some amazing things about her son Larry. "When he was around two, he would react to small one-engine-type airplanes by lying down spread-eagled on the ground. There is a small airport near our house. Whenever my husband or I were taking him for a walk and one of those small planes came overhead, Larry would react this way and then get up and resume his walk, as if nothing had happened." Apparently, the little boy only reacted this way with small one-engine planes; ordinary large airplanes, jets, did not disturb him in the least. He would merely point at them and say, plane, like any other little boy.

However, by the time Larry reached age three things crystallized somewhat more. "He started to talk about the war with Germany, about the soldiers in their green uniforms," Mrs. Killela explained. "He told us, at age three, how he killed his best friend by not helping him, and how he broke his leg on a large rock. He said he was taken away in a four-passenger ambulance. One evening we had pumpernickel bread at supper and Larry pointed at it saying it was black bread and that they ate it with fish soup. Periodically he brought up different things and made comments. We never prompted him or started deliberate conversations about it." Mrs. Killela had no idea what color uniforms the Germans wore in World War II. One day she read a book about the war and learned that the Germans wore green uniforms.

Mrs. Killela also noticed that whenever the little boy played war, as other children do, it was always the Germans and Americans. As Larry grew older, he did not refer to the things he "knew," but behaved more and more like any average boy his age. The Killelas assumed quite correctly that the four-passenger ambulance referred to by the little boy must have been a military one, and that the small one-engine planes reminded the little boy of fighter planes.

Gloria Smith, who lives in New York State, has a twenty-year-old daughter. When the little girl was three years old, an incident occurred that made Mrs. Smith wonder whether her child wasn't speaking of reincarnation memories. The family was watching television at the time and it so happened that a program dealing with Pilgrims was on the screen. Unexpectedly, the little girl said, "My other mommie wore clothes like that." Mrs. Smith was quite surprised and asked her daughter to repeat the statement. Firmly the little girl replied, "The mother I used to have wore dresses like that." There wasn't anything else Mrs. Smith could get out of the child, but the little girl insisted again and again that she had had another mother, and that she was dressed in clothes similar to those she was seeing on television.

Mrs. H. P. Zieschang of Ohio is now well into her eighties. When she was a little girl, she frequently broke into tears and asked to go to see her other parents. This was a repeated occurrence, and the child, at the time, insisted that she wanted to go back to the parents *she knew*. Eventually, the desire faded as the child grew older. But to this day Mrs. Zieschang can draw a picture of her previous home and its surroundings and the little girl she used to be. Connected with this was a strong feeling of having lived in the old South. "I can't drive through certain portions of the South without looking for the one I used to live in," Mrs. Zieschang explained. "Also, one day I was standing on our porch looking out, enjoying the trees, when all at once I was standing in the doorway of a little log cabin, looking across a tiny clearing at a primeval forest and smelling the fragrance of the trees. It was a brief flash and then I was back on my own porch."

Ordinary memories fade in time, and so it is not surprising that reincarnation memories might also fade as time goes on. It is therefore rather interesting to study the cases of young children who have such memories, which in later life will disappear from their conscious minds. A good case in point was brought to my attention recently by Mrs. Carole Hardin, in Montana. Mrs. Hardin lives with her husband, who works in one of the local mines. She is an art student by correspondence, and they are people in the middle-income bracket—ordinary people, I would say, living in an eight-year-old country house. They have four children— nine, seven, four, and three years of age—representative of an average middle-class family. Mrs. Hardin has a crippling condition that prevents her from writing in longhand. Other than that, there really isn't anything extraordinary about them. There is, however, a great deal to be said about one of their children, Brenda, aged four.

Nothing very special happened with little Brenda until Good Friday of 1969. On that day, Brenda sat up, awaking from a sound sleep, and started to talk about a previous life. She had spent the night in the home of Mrs. Hardin's sister, Mrs. Perry.

"I have lived in the country once," the little girl said, "in the South, in a big white house." She then went on to describe it as having had a big porch with white pillars and a big green lawn. She referred to a pet horse named Hooper John that she seemed rather fond of. Her aunt asked her if there were any other children. "Yes," the little girl said, "a lot of little darkies." She spoke with a strong accent, apparently French, and even gave her name, which was also a French name. Her aunt couldn't even pronounce it. Finally, the little girl added, "But I died." Her aunt thought she had misunderstood her and asked what she had said. "I died," the little girl repeated somewhat impatiently, "I fell off my horse, Hooper John, when I was sixteen, and died." She then lay back down and went back to sleep. The little girl's uncle, Mr. Perry, who was present throughout this amazing conversation, attributed it all to the child's lively imagination, but the following morning the aunt again spoke to little Brenda when she awoke.

Present this time was her daughter Sharon, aged fourteen. Together the two questioned the little girl further: Did she live on a farm when she lived down South? "Of course not," the little girl said, "it was a plantation." She then went on to describe how they raised tobacco, speaking of cutting the tobacco and sheaves. When asked what it looked like, she said, "You know, like crimped tobacco." Brenda then repeated the same account she had told for the first time the previous night. She spoke of a fire wagon, described a firebox and the purpose it served, but as the day wore on she forgot about this, being, after all, only four years old. By evening she had completely forgotten the incident. However, a few days later she referred to a toy horse as "Hooper John" for just a moment, finally saying, "Oh, no, you're not my Hooper John." She put the toy down and has not spoken of it ever since.

Now, this is an extraordinary thing for a four-year-old girl to use phrases, language, and information rarely, if ever, possessed by someone that young; especially so since Brenda had had no occasion to visit the South or to learn about the tobacco business. At age four, most children do not read books, nor has Mrs. Hardin read any such stories to her at any time.

*

CHAPTER TEN

The Perfect Case
for Reincarnation:
Scotland 1600

ONE DAY IN OCTOBER OF 1967, I was going through my fan mail, which had been piling up for a few weeks. I get about three to four hundred letters a week from readers all over the country, and even from abroad, and I cannot devote as much time to these letters as I wish I could, but on this brisk October morning I felt compelled to go over the mail and to try to pick out the most urgent letters for an immediate reply. Somehow my hands picked up a letter from Harvey, Illinois. It looked just like any other letter that I might get from a reader but I proceeded to open it and read it. I read it three times, and then I wondered what had made me open this particularl letter of all the hundreds that lay on my desk that morning.

> Dear Mr. Holzer,
>
> I am writing to you about an experience I had, which may not really mean anything. I have seen what looks like a Scottish girl, standing at the foot of my bed, three times. I don't know if she actually talked to me, but after I'd seen her, these words keep coming back to me: "castle," "perch" or "purth," "Ruthvin," "Cowrye," "sixteen," and "towers." Also, something which sounds like "burn night." I've never mentioned this to anyone, because they probably would not believe me.

If you can make anything out of this, I would appreciate it if you would let me know.

Sincerely,

Pamela Wollenberg.

What puzzled me about this short letter was the fact that the words mentioned by Miss Wollenberg had no immediate meaning for me either. It didn't sound like the usual ghost story or the usual psychic experience relating simply to something left behind in the atmosphere of a particular room or house. It didn't sound like an ordinary dream either, since Miss Wollenberg was not precise in mentioning what appeared to be place names.

I was intrigued by her letter, and I wrote back requesting additional information, asking her whether she could remember any more details about this girl or any further communications from her.

The lady from Harvey, Illinois, answered my letter immediately. I had asked her whether there were any witnesses to the experience she had reported in her first letter, but apparently there weren't any, since she was asleep at the time.

I have no witnesses to the Scottish girl I see, because no one else has seen her. The girl I see seems to have red hair and seems to be very elegantly dressed, with long white gown and gold braid. I saw her the other night. It seems she said to me the word "handsel." It seems as though she's lost. She keeps saying "ruthven," "gowrie," "sixteen hundred," "two towers." She also said, "glamis—angus." She also said, "I leaped." I don't believe I have any Scottish background, but it's possible, because on my mother's side they are all English. On my father's side they are all German. I do not know if I have ESP, but I seem to see some things before they happen.

I hope this will help you.

Sincerely,

Pamela Wollenberg.

The matter rested there for awhile, but I was determined to go to

Scotland in the future and investigate this material. It meant nothing to me at the time, but I knew some research historians in Scotland and thought that perhaps they might be able to shed some light on the mysterious words of Miss Wollenberg's letters.

We had no further correspondence until I was able to go to Scotland in the summer of 1969. I took the two letters with me, although I really didn't know where to begin the search. One of my dearest friends is a writer named Elizabeth Byrd, author of *Immortal Queen* (a history of Mary, Queen of Scots), who then resided in the Scottish Highlands. I thought that perhaps Elizabeth could shed some light on the material I was bringing along with me. She read the two letters, but could not offer anything concrete except the promise to look into it further.

We were luncheon guests of Mr. and Mrs. Maurice Simpson at their castle in northeastern Scotland, called Muchalls. The occasion was a casual invitation of the Simpsons to visit their castle because of a possible haunted room. It turned out that there was no such room, but the Simpsons were amiable people, whose hospitality we enjoyed.

For no reason in particular, I mentioned my letters from the lady in Harvey, Illinois, wondering whether Mr. Simpson had some idea as to the meaning of those letters. To my amazement, Mr. Simpson caught on immediately and seemed to remember a legend or story involving "a maiden's leap" in one of the castles in Scotland.

"You mean, there is something to this?" I said, getting more and more interested. Evidently, fate had destined us to come to Muchalls not because of a haunted room, but because of a link supplied by the owner, leading me to an understanding of what Miss Wollenberg's letter was all about.

"I think I have a guidebook here, a book dealing with Scottish castles," he said. "Let me look for it."

A few minutes later he returned, triumphantly holding what seemed to be a slender booklet. The booklet was called *Huntingtower Castle* and was the work of J. S. Richardson, formerly Inspector of Ancient Monuments for Scotland. Huntingtower Castle is now under the supervision of the Ministry of Public Building and Works. As I leafed through this booklet I realized that we had discovered the key to Pamela Wollenberg's strange dream/vision.

What is now called Huntingtower Castle was originally known as Ruthven Castle. The name goes back to the first half of the thirteenth century. The third and fourth Lords Ruthven apparently had some part in the murder of Rizzio, Queen Mary's favorite; and the father subsequently died while the son eventually returned from England, whence he had fled, and received a full royal pardon. This fourth Lord Ruthven, whose first name was William, was created the first Earl of Gowrie by King James in 1581. The king was then still legally an infant, and his regents actually created the title.

The following year the newly created earl repaid the favor in a rather peculiar fashion. He and some associates captured the young king and held him a prisoner for almost a year at Ruthven Castle. The reasons were political. Gowrie and his associates disapproved of the government of the Earl of Arran and the Duke of Lennox, who were then running Scotland. They took power away from those two nobles and into their own hands, with the young king unable to do much about it. They forced the king to listen to their complaints and to sign a declaration denouncing the former government. When the young man remonstrated against this enforced order, the master of Glamis, who was among those detaining the young king, is reported to have said, "Better bairns greet than bearded men," meaning, "Better a boy weeps than a bearded man!" Allegedly, King James never forgot those words.

This "Raid of Ruthven" was an important event in Scottish history; that is, important to those who specialize in sixteenth-century Scottish history and do research into this turbulent era.

Eventually, it appears, when King James found his freedom, he returned under the sway of the Earl of Arran, so the detention at Ruthven really didn't change anything, except, perhaps, the king's feelings toward the man he had just created the first Earl of Gowrie.

At first he showed a forgiving spirit to those who had been connected with the raid, for he issued a proclamation offering them all a full pardon. But two years later the Earl of Gowrie was ordered to leave the country. Having retired only to Dundee, he was arrested by one William Stewart, taken by ship to Leith, and thence to the royal palace of Holyrood. There he stood trial on the accusation of being implicated in a plot to seize Stirling Castle, was found guilty, and was beheaded at Stirling on May 4, 1585, his property being forfeited to the crown.

A year later, the estates and honors of the first earl were restored to his son James, who died, however, shortly after. He was succeeded in 1588 by his brother John, the third and last Earl of Gowrie. All the Gowries, incidentally, had the reputation in their time of being adepts of necromancy and witchcraft.

Evidently, King James's revenge did not stop there. The last Earl of Gowrie and his brother Alexander Ruthven were killed upon his orders in their Perth town house in August of 1600. The reason given at the time was "an alleged attempt on the life of the King," which was apparently without foundation. No details are known of this so-called "Gowrie conspiracy," but contemporary reports speak of some papers taken from the belt of the dead earl that contained magic spells no one but an adept in the black arts could properly read. The dead bodies of the two brothers were then carried to Edinburgh, where indictments for high treason were read publicly.

Not satisfied with having executed the two Ruthven brothers, the king ordered their bodies to be publicly hanged, drawn, and quartered, and the remnants to be distributed to various parts of Scotland, thus insuring, according to the belief of the times, that their souls could not rest in peace.

The early seventeenth century was a hard and rough period in history. People were not gentle to each other, and political tempers rose high at times. Religious differences had not been settled, and Scotland was torn by the Protestant and Catholic factions. The king's continuing vengefulness must be understood against this violent background. The Parliament of 1600 abolished the name of Ruthven, ordering that the castle change its name to Huntingtower and remain a property of the Crown of Scotland. Finally, in 1643, the castle passed into the hands of William Murray and was generally known from that time onward only as Huntingtower Castle.

It required the knowledge and skill of a Scottish historical specialist to recall the earlier designation as Ruthven Castle and the connection between the names Ruthven and Gowrie, and yet a young lady who had never left her native Illinois was able to speak of Ruthven and Gowrie and the year 1600 and the two towers, all in one and the same breath. She was even able to speak of Glamis and

Angus, not realizing the connection between the master of Glamis, which is in Angus County, and the Gowrie family. How could she know that Perth, which was mentioned in her very first letter to me, was the place where the Earl of Gowrie was slain?

But Pamela Wollenberg had also written, "I leaped." Again, the official Huntingtower Castle booklet was able to give me some clues as to the meaning of this cryptic remark:

> A daughter of the first Earl of Gowrie was courted by a young gentleman of inferior rank, whose intentions were not countenanced by the family. When a visitor at the castle, he was always lodged in a separate tower from the young lady. One night, however, before the doors were shut, she conveyed herself into her lover's apartment, but some prying duenna acquainted the Countess with it, who, cutting off, as she thought, all possibility of retreat, hastened to surprise them. The young lady's ears were quick. She heard the footsteps of the old Countess, ran to the top of the leads, and took the desperate leap of nine feet four inches, over a chasm of sixty feet, and luckily landing on the battlements of the other tower, crept into her own bed, where her astonished mother found her, and, of course, apologized for her unjust suspicion. The fair daughter did not choose to repeat the leap, but the next night eloped and was married. This extraordinary exploit has given the name of "the maiden's leap" to the space between the two towers, which were originally separate.

After I had read the contents of the official booklet, there was a moment of silence when we all realized the importance of the information contained therein.

What remained to be found was further corroboration of the material—perhaps some knowledge concerning the further events of the Gowrie conspiracy itself, and the girl's name. All this had to be investigated further, but at least I knew then that Pamela Wollenberg either had authentic experiences reaching out into an earlier time or there had to be a logical explanation for her knowledge. I decided not to tell Miss Wollenberg anything whatsoever about my research, but to arrange for an early meeting with her so that we could begin hypnotic regression. At this point I knew nothing whatsoever about Miss Wollenberg, nor even her age or status, and I could only hope that there would be no reason why she could not submit to the experiment I intended to undertake.

Also present at the delightful dinner at Muchalls were Mr. and Mrs. Alastair Knight. Mrs. Knight, whose first name is Alanna, is highly psychic. She is a writer of historical novels, and offered to help me research this unusual case. In addition, Elizabeth Byrd enlisted the voluntary aid of historian Carson Ritchie, but Mr. Ritchie made it plain to her that finding girls' names is a difficult matter. In those days, girls' births were not registered unless they were royal.

Fortified by such a formidable team of helpers, I was confident I could crack the mystery of Pamela Wollenberg's strange visions. The Knights decided to go to Gowrie Castle at the very first opportunity.

Two phrases in Pamela's original vision had not yet been fully explained or placed. There was, first of all, the expression "burn night." *Burn* is Scottish for brook. Far more interesting is the word *handsel*. The term seemed completely unfamiliar to me. Where was I to find an explanation for this strange word?

Through Elizabeth Byrd, I had met authoress Margaret Widdemer some years before. Elizabeth asked for permission to consult Miss Widdemer, who is widely read and who had a fine research library. "From my Chambers' *Scottish Dictionary*," Miss Widdemer wrote, "I can give you an explanation for 'Handsel': an inaugural gift, a present, on Handsel Monday, a coin put in the pocket of a new coat or the like. Handsel means to inaugurate, to make a beginning, a gift." I was, of course, elated at this news that there was such a word as *handsel*. Miss Widdemer had an opinion of her own. "My first reaction to the word was earnest money, or something given as a sealing of a bargain, money or not. Possibly the red-haired girl you speak of was Handselled to the man she leaped to." So there was such a word after all.

More and more pieces of the jigsaw puzzle began to fall into place now, even though I had not yet met Miss Pamela Wollenberg in person. Mr. and Mrs. Knight prepared for a visit to Gowrie Castle on my behalf. This came about in a most unusual way. On August 6, they found themselves on a routine trip connected with Mr. Knight's work as a geologist. They were looking for Scone Palace and having a hard time finding it, so they decided to go instead to visit a relative in Dundee. They decided to take a short cut but suddenly found themselves completely lost, and after a bewildering number of side roads, halted at a signpost reading HUNTINGTOWER CASTLE—TWO MILES. It was only much later that they realized that they had arrived at what had once been Gowrie Castle, on the anniversary of the execution of the last two Gowrie lords.

Now, Alanna Knight does not take her psychic abilities too seriously, although I have seen her at work using her sixth sense to good advantage. She is apparently able to pierce the veil of time and to relive events in the distant past. As soon as they arrived at the castle, she experienced a strange sense of familiarity. The moment she set foot into Huntingtower Castle she was sure she had been in it before, except that she knew it when it was furnished. Her husband assured her that they had never been there. Suddenly, Mrs. Knight knew her way inside.

"This was a bedroom. The bed was over there," she said and pointed. As she went from room to room she found herself singing under her breath. Her son Christopher asked, "What is it that you are singing?" She couldn't tell him, but it was the same tune that had been running through her mind ever since I had mentioned I had written a song entitled "The Maid in the Meadow." Mrs. Knight has never heard my song nor has she seen any sheet music of it. All she knew was that I had written such a song and that there was some connection with Scotland. When they came across the custodian of the castle, she immediately asked her about Ruthven Field Meadow, as it is marked on the map. Following the custodian's directions, they meandered along some pretty lanes, which again seemed rather too familiar to her. Her feelings of déjà vu were rather vague, and yet, at the same time, they were definite.

When they started to leave the area and her husband wondered how they would get out of there, having been lost once that afternoon, she immediately replied, "About twenty yards further on there is an old stone bridge on the right, which leads to the main road eventually," and there was. As they drove away, she could not help but go over the events of the last hour in her mind.

Once inside the castle she had immediately gone up to the battlements, practically on hands and knees, as the steps were very steep. There she had perched on the edge of the battlements, about sixty feet above ground. Today the two original towers, which were separate at one time, are connected by a somewhat lower central portion. In the early seventeenth century, however, there was a chasm between the two portions of the castle measuring over nine feet. Anyone wishing to leap from the right-hand tower onto the lower, left-hand tower would still have to cover a distance of nine feet. But since the left-hand portion was one story below the right-hand portion, the leap would have been downward. Also, there is a ledge along both battlements, and as the buttresses protrude and overlap, it reduces the distance by a couple of feet. Thus it is not entirely impossible to make such a leap safely and without falling off the roof, but it is somewhat of a feat, just the same. Eventually, Alanna Knight had left the battlement and returned to the inside of the castle.

In what she considers a bedroom, she had had a very strong impression of a girl with reddish-gold hair, pale rather than dark, with freckles. She was what, in modern parlance, would be called a tomboy, Alanna reports—mischievous rather than passionately amorous. "The sort of girl who would do anything for a dare," Alanna felt, "and who would enjoy leading a man on, feeling rather superior to the poor creature. I think she was merry, laughed a lot, was strongly disapproved of by her family. I feel that the sixteenth century wasn't her time; she was a misplacement and would have been happier living now, who even then yearned for some equality with men, and watched them go out to fight with envy in her soul. I think also that her name is Margaret or Isabelle or both, but these names are particularly Scottish, so there is really nothing exciting about this feeling. I only hope that one day you'll know the answer."

I asked Alanna Knight about the song that kept going through her mind and that she felt had something to do with my ballad "The Maid of the Meadow." Since she is not a musician, she asked a friend, Ann Brand, to transcribe it for her. I looked at the musical composition with interest. There are four bars, and they resemble greatly four bars from my ballad, written in 1953, and unknown to Alanna Knight or her friend. To be sure, it wasn't the entire song; it was merely a portion of it, but the similarity was striking.

Alanna had one other bit of news to add: Dr. Ritchie had found some reference to one of the Ruthven girls. In Robertson's

History of Scotland, published in 1759, he had found a reference to
the sister of the Earl of Gowrie by the name of Mistress Beatrix. Of
course, there might have been more than one sister but the name
is on record. In the meantime, Elizabeth Byrd had promised further inquiries in Edinburgh.

While all this feverish activity on my behalf was going on
across the ocean, I went to Chicago to finally meet Pamela Wollenberg in person. She had agreed to come to the Knickerbocker
Hotel, where I was then staying, and to submit to hypnotic regression. I had told her that I had found some interesting evidence
relating to her dream vision but declined to say anymore.

On October 17, 1969, Pamela Wollenberg came to my suite at
the Knickerbocker Hotel. When she entered I was somewhat surprised, for she didn't look at all like the person I had somehow
imagined her to be. Instead of a fey, somewhat romantic individual
of indeterminate age, I found her to be a young girl of twenty or
twenty-one, lively and practical, and not at all interested in the
occult. I explained that I would interview her first and then attempt to put her into hypnotic regression. Since she was agreea-
ble, we proceeded immediately.

In the following pages I am presenting the exact transcript of
our interview and of what happened when Pamela Wollenberg
became another person.

"Pamela," I began the conversation, "where were you born?"

"Chicago Heights."

"What does your father do?"

"My father is deceased. He worked in a factory which built
locomotives, and my mother works in a hospital as a dietary
worker."

"What is your background?"

"My father's family are from Germany, the Black Forest, and
my mother's side of the family are English."

"Was she born here?"

"Yes."

"Is there anybody of Scottish ancestry among your family?"

"Not that I know of."

"Do you have any brothers and sisters?"

"I have half sisters and a half brother."

"What is your family's religion?"

"Well, my father's side of the family is Lutheran, and my mother's family is Baptist."

"And you, yourself?"

"I consider myself a Mormon."

"You're twenty-one. Do you work?"

"I was doing work in a hospital. I was going to nursing school, and now I'm just taking care of a woman part time. She's ill, and once I get the money I want to go back into nursing."

"What is your schooling like? What did you do? You went to public school?"

"I went to school in Glenwood, right outside of Chicago Heights, and the rest of my schooling was all in Harvey, where I live now."

"Did you ever have any flashes or visions or feelings of having been in places that you hadn't really visited?"

"I've seen people that I'd swear that I'd seen somewhere before, and no possibility of it."

"Have you ever been to Europe?"

"No."

"Have you ever had any desire to go to Europe?"

"Oh, yes, I'd love to go to Europe. I want to see castles."

"When did you first notice this desire?"

"Oh, I'd say maybe three years ago, when I was eighteen."

"Do you know the first time you had this sudden desire to see castles?"

"I had a castle, all in my mind—a big, white castle with towers."

"How many towers?"

"Two or three, I think, and it was like up on a stone, a mountain or something."

"What kind of books do you read?"

"Well, I read a lot of mysteries."

"Do you read any history?"

"No, history doesn't really interest me too much. I read about Waterloo one time, but that's about the first one I read."

"What kind of music do you like?"

"Classical music and folk songs. I don't mean folk songs like you hear now. I mean of the European countries, the British Isles."

"Do you ever have a particular song running through your mind?"

"I hear bagpipes sometimes."

"When do you hear these bagpipes?"

"Usually at night, when I'm getting ready to go to sleep."

"How long has that been going on?"

"I would say off and on now for maybe a year and a half, two years."

"Have you ever had a feeling of strangeness in your present surroundings?"

"Yes, I'd say so. I don't think I've ever belonged *around here.*"

"Can you be more specific as to when this feeling started?"

"I would say I've noticed it for the last couple of years, two or three years, possibly, but I don't really feel like I know anybody here. It seems I know people that are in other places of the world, and I *don't.*"

"What places would you say they are at?"

"Well, I think I'm really drawn more to the British Isles than I am to Europe. There's just something about the British Isles that fascinates me."

"Have you ever had a feeling, perhaps when you were very tired, of looking in the mirror or walking, seeing yourself *different* from what you look like now, see any change in yourself, personality, character, or in face?"

"Yes, I know one time I can remember very, very clearly, because it startled me. The girl that I talked about in the dream I had, with the red hair—I looked in the mirror one day—I don't know if I pictured myself *as her,* or if I saw her there, but it set me back."

"How long ago was that?"

"Oh, I'd say maybe nine months ago."

"Is that the only time you had this feeling?"

"I have had the feeling that I'm somebody besides who I am."

"How long have you had this feeling?"

"I'd have to go back two or three years."

"Anything, do you think, that started it off?"

"No, not that I can think of."

"Now, let us talk about the dreams."

"The dream happened the first time about two years ago. I've had it quite a few times since then. I've seen a girl with red hair. She has a long, white gown on, and it has gold braiding on it, and she's kind of walking like she's dazed. When I have this dream I also see two towers there, and I hear her say, 'Handsel to me,' and then I hear her mention 'Glamis, Angus,' and she'll say, 'Ruthven, Gowrie,' and one time she said, 'I leaped.' Sometimes she seems very peaceful, and sometimes she seems very angry."

"How old a girl would you say?"

"I'd say somewhere around twenty."

"Is she short or tall?"

"I would say short, somewhat petite."

"Pretty, ugly, anything special about her?"

"No, nothing really. She has beautiful red hair. That's the thing."

"Short or long?"

"Long hair, very thick."

"Does the dream vary at all or is it exactly the same each time?"

"I will say it is basically exactly the same every time, except there's times when she'll seem angry."

"How many times have you had the dream all together?"

"I'd say five or six times."

"When was the last time?"

"The last time, let's see, July, I think."

"Of this year?"

"Yes."

"Was she angry then?"

"Very angry."

"Do these dreams last all night, or are they short dreams?"

"Very short. I mean, I'll just see her and she'll say what she has to say, and then she's gone."

"How is it that you remember this particular dream so vividly? Do you remember all your dreams as well?"

"Her I do, because I'm not really sure if you can classify it as a dream. I don't really think I'm asleep."

"Does it happen early in the night, middle of the night, or late at night?"

"I would say after eleven-thirty and before two to two-thirty."

"Outside of those dreams, did you have any feeling of a presence around you in any way? While awake, I mean?"

"I don't know if I can say specifically *her* or not, but I have had the feeling at times that *someone's* around me. I mean, when I'm home by myself."

"When you contacted me, do you think that someone made you do it?"

"I felt I just *had* to write you, for no reason."

"Did it make any sense to you, personally?"

"The only thing I ever really thought about was the 'Handsel to me.' I thought the 'to me' must mean something. Maybe 'Handsel' means come to me, but I wouldn't know why she'd want me coming to her."

"Have you any particular tastes in clothes, accessories, music, habits, phrases—anything you find is alien to your own personality, especially since you were eighteen, let us say?"

"I love to cook anything which is from the English Isles. I have three English cookbooks. As for clothes, the old-style dress really appeals to me."

"Do you have any boyfriends who are of English or Scottish background? I don't mean American English, but I mean true native."

"No, none whatsoever."

"Have you ever done any reading about Britain to any extent—history, background, geography?"

"I read one time about the Tower of London, and I've read about the royal family, but really nothing else."

"What is your own view of the meaning of these phenomena that have occurred in you life? What do you suppose it means?"

"I don't really know, unless someone's trying to tell me something. I feel that I know her. I don't know *how* I know her or *why* I know her, but I feel *I know her.*"

"When the first dream occurred, the very first time, was it out of the blue? There was nothing that would indicate any reason for it?"

"The first time I really didn't pay much attention to it. I noticed it, and I knew it was there, but I thought, 'Well, one of these wild things,' but then it kept coming back, and every time it would come back I'd feel closer to her."

"Are you ready to be hypnotically regressed now?"

"Yes, I am."

A few moments later, Pamela was in deep hypnosis, fully relaxed, and obeying my commands. "You are going to go back a hundred years, two hundred years, three hundred years. Go back until you see the redheaded girl."

After a moment, she spoke.

"Ruthven . . .," she said quietly.

"Do you live there?" I began my questioning.

"I live there."

"Who is your father?"

"He's not there."

"Is there anyone else there?"

"My mother."

"What is her name? What is your mother's name?"

"I don't know. We can't talk about it."

"Why not?"

"Because they're conspiring against us, and we're not supposed to talk about them."

"What year are we in?"

"Sixteen hundred."

"Sixteen hundred what?"

"Just sixteen hundred."

"What country do you live in?"

"In Scotland."

"Why are you worried?"

"We're going to have to leave."

"Why do you have to leave?"

"They'll kill us if we don't leave."

"Who will kill you?"

"I don't know. Father just said, 'the men.'"

"What are you going to do?"

"I don't know. Mother's packing."

"Where are you going to go?"

"To Glamis."

"Why there?"

"The royal family is there."

"Will they help you?"

"I don't know."

"Describe your home."

"Stones."

"What is it called?"

"Breasten."

"What does the building look like?"

"Two towers, garden."

"Have you been up in the towers?"

"I used to play up there."

"How did you play?"

"I had little china cups."

"How old were you then?"

"Four, five."

"How old are you now?"

"Twenty-two."

"Are you single or married?"

"Single."

"Do you know any man you would like to marry?"

"Yes."

"What is his name?"

"I can't tell his name."

"Why not?"

"I'm not supposed to see him."

"Why not?"

"The family says no."

"What is his first name?"

"Mother said I'll be punished if I tell."

"And what will you do? Have you seen him lately?"

"Yes."

"Where?"

"By Loch Catherine."

"Is that far away?"

"Not too far."

"Has he ever been in the castle?"

"Yes."

"Where? In what part of it?"

"In the main hallway."

"Never upstairs?"

"Only once, but he's not allowed in the castle."

"Was he upstairs in the tower at any time?"

"Only once, when Mother wasn't supposed to know he was there."

"What did you do?"

"We talked."

"And will you marry him?"

"I can't."

"Why not?"

"The family won't allow it. They want me to marry someone else."

"Who?"

"I don't know him."

"Why do they want you to marry this other person?"

"The family is very wealthy."

"And your friend isn't?"

"Yes, but not to their wealth."

"Why is it that you have come to speak through this instrument? What is your connection with her? Are you her or are you speaking *through* her?"

"I am *her.*"

"Where have you been in between? Have you been anyone else?"

"No, I was caught in the wind."

"How did you die?"

"I jumped from the tower."

"Did you die in jumping?"

"Yes, I died after."

"Where did you jump to?"

"I was trying to jump to the other one."

"Didn't you make it?"

"No."

"Where did you fall?"

"In front of the door."

"Was that the first time that you ever jumped from one tower to the other?"

"No."

"You've done it before?"

"Yes."

"And it worked?"

"Yes."

"And this time it didn't, and you died? How old were you then?"

"Twenty-two."

"Was it an accident, or did you want to jump?"

"I wanted to jump."

"Were you unhappy?"

"Yes."

"When you were down there dead, what happened to you next? What did you see next?"

"Nothing."

"What was your next memory after you had fallen? What is the next thing that you remember?"

"I was in wind."

"Did you see yourself as you were?"

"Yes."

"Where did you go?"

"Nowhere."

"Did you see anyone?"

"No."

"Did you stay outside or did you return to the castle?"

"I went to the castle once."

"Did anyone see you?"

"No."

"And what happened after that? Where did you live?"

"I was caught in the wind again."

"And what was the next thing you remember after that?"

"I saw people."

"What sort of people?"

"Funny people walking around."

"Were they also dead?"

"No."

"Where were you?"

"I was in a city."

"Were you in another body?"

"No."

"You were still as you were?"

"Yes."

"What was the city?"

"I don't know."

"Were the people dressed in the same way as the people you knew in your time?"

"No."

"Were you the same way as you were in your time?"

"Yes, I could see my gown."

"These funny people—did they notice you?"

"No, they walked by me."

"What was the next thing you remember after that?"

"I wanted someone to take me back."

"Back where?"

"To Ruthven."

"Did you find anyone?"

"Yes—Pamela."

"How did she take you back?"

"She'll take me back."

"How did you get *into* Pamela? Did you select her yourself?"

"Yes, she looked like she'd go back."

"Who told you about Pamela? How did you find her?"

"I found her when I went into the building."

"Which building?"

"In her building."

"But, what makes you so sure that she can?"

"She'll feel sorry and take me back."

"Are you within her? Are you in her body?"

"Yes, I've got to go back with her."

"Who sent you to her?"

"No one."

"Then how did you know where to find her?"

"I don't know."

"Did you talk to anyone and ask for help?"

"No one could hear me. They walked right by."

"There was no one, no person who said, 'You must go back to earth,' or anything like that?"

"No."

"Do you remember being reborn as a baby?"

"No."

"What was the thing you remember after you saw Pamela?"

"She looks like someone."

"Like who? Does she look like you?"

"No."

"Then what does she look like to you?"

"She looks like the clan McGibbon."

"Which one of the clan McGibbon?"

"She looks like Catherine."

"Catherine of the clan McGibbon? Who was Catherine to you?"

"I didn't know her too well. I met her only in Angus."

"Why did you go to Angus?"

"We had to go to Glamis."

"And did you pass through Angus?"

"No, Glamis is in Angus."

"What was she doing in Glamis?"

"She lives there."

"What does she do there?"

"A maid."

"Whose maid was she?"

"At the castle of the royal family."

"And Pamela reminds you of her?"

"Yes."

"But, what is it that binds you to Pamela? Is it your own destiny?"

"Yes, I must go back."

"And do what?"

"I've got to look for something."

"What do you have to look for?"

"My ring."

"Who gave you the ring?"

"I can't talk about it."

"What does it look like?"

"It's round, an opal."

"Is there anything inscribed in it?"

"No."

"Why is it so important to get this ring?"

"*He* gave it to me."

"Who did?"

"I'd be punished if I tell."

"You will not be punished . . . on my honor. Give me his name so I can help you."

"I can't find him again. I only want my ring."

"Call out for him, and he will come to you."

"I'll be punished if I tell."

"And when you find the ring, what will you do then?"

"I'll go away."

"Where will you go to?"

"Loch Catherine. I was happy there."

"With whom?"

"*He* would take me there. We would talk about going away."

"Where would you go to, if you could?"

"Away from Perth."

"And where to?"

"He'd like to go to London."

"What sort of work does he do?"

"He wants to be an architect."

"Has he studied?"

"Only a little, but without permission."

"He's not a nobleman?"

"He's a nobleman, but his father does not want him to do that."

"Why is it that you came to Pamela when she was about eighteen and not before?"

"She's old enough to go away now."

"Will you help her go there? Why did you seek *me* out?"

"Maybe you would make her go."

"Is that what you want me to do?"

"I want to go back."

"Suppose I promise to help you, will you then tell me who the young man was?"

"Can I go back?"

"I will try to find a way for her to go back, yes. I have already made contact over there, and I know you are telling the truth."

"Will she take me back?"

"I will do my best for her to take you back within a year's time."

"I've waited too long."

"How long have you waited?"

"For hundreds of years."

"Then you can wait another year. But a lot of time has gone on. Perhaps the ring isn't there anymore. Then what?"

"I'll look till I find it."

"Are you happy being in Pamela's person now? Are you reconciled to being her? Do you like being her?"

"Only to go back."

"I am still curious why it is, and how it is, that you found her over here. Do you know in what country you are? Do you?"

"No."

"Where do you think you are? Do you know the name of the country in which you are? It is not Scotland."

"I'm not in the Isles?"

"No. Do you know how much time has gone on since you lived? Do you know how much?"

"Hundreds of years."

"Do you want to tell me the name of the young man?"

"I can't have him again. You won't bring him back."

"Tell me more about this conspiracy that frightened you so. Who was involved?"

"Father just said they were against him."

"Who?"

"I only know him as Gowrie."

"What rank did he have?"

"I don't know. When they came, I had to go to the tower."

"And when they called for you, what name did they use?"

"I want him back!"

"I will help you. You can tell me your name now, your true name."

"I have to look in the Bible."

"Go and look at the Bible and tell me what is written in it."

"No, I have to go see him."

"You will see him, if he *wants* you to see him."

"No, I want Peter."

"Peter shall be yours. I have promised it. Now, your name."

"I want Peter."

"Peter, come to her. If you have been reborn, let her know where you are, so that she may come to you again. You have to say, 'I,' and say your name, 'want you.' Then he will come to you."

"We can't tell any people."

"You and I are the only ones to know."

"No; when we left the castle, Mother said, 'No.'"

"Speak your name."

"No, I'll be hit."

"What did the servants call you?"

"They always called me by my proper name of Ruthven."

"But what did they say when they meant you were there?"

"They called me 'Lady.'"

"Lady what? What is your Christian name?"

"I can't."

"You know it?"

"Yes."

"What is the initial? The first letter of your name?"

"I'll be punished."

"You will not be punished to speak your own name."

"I can't tell you."

"You would like to find the ring. Is there anything else you want?"

"No."

"Then will you be at peace? If you find the ring, or when you find there is no more ring, will you be at peace then?"

"Yes, if I may go to the Loch."

"Alone?"

"Yes."

"Be patient, and I will see whether it can be done. Have you any other requests?"

"No."

"If I ask you a question, will you answer it truthfully? Do you promise to answer it truthfully?"

"Yes."

"Are you *Beatrix?*"

"I can't tell you."

"You must say yes or no."

"But I'll be punished."

"You will not be punished, because you are not *telling* me. You are simply saying yes or no. If you say yes and it is the truth, you will not have said it; and if you say no and it is the truth, you will have perjured yourself and lied and invited damnation. So you had better tell the truth. For the third and last time, I ask you, *are you Lady Beatrix?*"

"Yes."

"I will now release you, and I will see to it that as soon as it is possible, you shall see your favorite place again."

"Yes."

"Then go in peace with my blessing."

After Pamela woke up, remembering absolutely nothing of her hypnotic regression, I asked her how she happened to get the name Pamela in the first place.

"My mother couldn't decide on a name and she wanted a name no one in the family had and she read a society page and there was a girl by the name of Pamela being married."

"I'm going to name a few women's names. Tell me if any of them rings a bell in some way or means anything special, all right? Dorothy or Dorothea."

"My grandmother is named Dorothy.'

"You like that name?"

"It's all right."

"How about Barbara?"

"No."

"How about Beatrix?"

"That's pretty. *I like that.*"

"You like that better than the others?"

"Yes, as long as people didn't call me Bea. I don't care for that."

The material obtained from Pamela while in hypnotic regression was very interesting indeed. Now I knew what the *handsel* was: the ring that meant so much to her because of the one who had given it to her. When I realized that she wasn't going to give me her name, it was best to try to see what reaction I might get from her by mentioning several names. Although I do not consider the evidence thus obtained in the same light as spontaneous admission of facts or names, it is nevertheless of interest in the context of this entire investigation that she did react to the name Beatrix significantly differently from the reaction to other names mentioned by me in the same tone of voice.

After awhile, Pamela sat up and joined me for a cup of coffee. Only then did I open the latest letter from Elizabeth Byrd, which had reached me the day before in New York. In it was enclosed a communication from the Lord Lyon of Scotland; that is to say, the nobleman in charge of registering claims and coats of arms of noble families.

> The daughter after which the maiden's leap at Huntingtower was named was Dorothea, who married before June 8, 1609, John Wemyss, of Pittencrieff. Dorothea, however, though the thirteenth child, was not apparently the youngest daughter, and information on Barbara, the fourteenth child and youngest of that family, can be found on pages 266 and 267 of Volume Four of the Scots Peerage, referred to above.

Thus read the report from the Lord Lyon of Scotland. Of course, the list of Gowrie daughters is by no means complete. A further thought entered my mind. True, Pamela in her other identity as Lady Gowrie had spoken of leaping, but was she the one for whom the Maiden's Leap was famous? Could she not have been another person, peaking and falling where another had leaped and landed safely? On reexamining the testimony, it appears to me that the Lady Gowrie who spoke to me in Chicago, and who fell to her death from the battlements of Gowrie Castle, was not in the habit of practicing the leap to reach her love, but then again, the true evidence may be confused. Nigel Tranter, in his book *The Fortified House in Scotland,* speaks only of the battlements and the buildings themselves, so the legend of the Maiden's Leap was not as far-spread as we might think.

Before I parted company with Pamela Wollenberg, I asked that she observe anything that might happen to her after our hypnosis session. In particular, I then asked that she record any dream/visions that she might have in the future; for it is possible that a memory can be stirred up as a consequence of hypnotic regression.

Four days after our meeting, I received a letter from Pamela. Now, I had briefly told her that her Scottish memories had been confirmed by experts, and that she apparently had lived once before as one of the ladies Gowrie. Thus, anything duplicating that which she already knew would be of no evidential value, of course.

> I don't know if this will mean anything or not, but I felt compelled to write you. It's almost 2:30 A.M., but I have just

awoken from a dream which seems very real to me. In my dream I found myself on a horse in a place I don't know, but still I feel I know it. I started riding, and after about forty miles or so I stopped and tied my horse to a tree. I started walking in what seemed to be a valley, and it was very wooded. I also saw mountains around me. As I was walking, there were thorns, or something sharp scratching my leg. I started to approach a river, and then I began running. After that I found myself in bed again, and the thing that startled me most is that I felt the most terrible burning sensation on my legs. Then I was taken back by the most awful crying and moaning sounds, which I thought would awaken the entire neighborhood.

Two words have impressed themselves strongly onto my mind. One is either "dab" or "daba." I don't know where it came from, but it's been bothering me. The other word is "Beitris," which I saw clearly on the ceiling of my room last night, with the lights turned off. I don't know if all this will mean anything or not, but I had to write you.

Since the words did not have any meaning for me either, I asked Elizabeth Byrd to check them out in Jamison's *English-Scottish Dictionary. Daddown* means to fall forcibly and with noise. Did the term have reference to her fatal fall from the battlements of Gowrie Castle? But there is also *dablet* which means an imp, a little devil. Didn't Alanna Knight describe the girl she saw in her visions as something of that sort?

In early November Pamela had another dream/vision. The same image impressed itself upon her mind twice in a row, and she was a little worried about the message it contained.

"You will die by *Newa Vleen*," the girl said in the dreams. Pamela wondered *who* was to die—the redhead or herself—and what, if anything, did Newa Vleen signify?

On April 30, 1972, I received a letter from Mrs. A. McDougall, who lives in Perth, Scotland, shedding some intriguing light on the authenticity of Pamela's statements:

The girl in question was the daughter of the fourth Lord Ruthven who was married to Lord Methven's daughter whose family name was Stewart and she was Lady Dorothea Stewart. He was given the title of the Earl of Gowrie after he and Lord

Lindsay had escorted Queen Mary to Loch Leven and extorted a commission from her which empowered them to overthrow the government in her name.

The young daughter who made the now famous leap, eloped with her lover Squire James Wemyss of Pittencrieff, which is almost adjacent to Loch Katrine, in the Trossachs.

The word Newavleen is quite possibly of Jacobite origin which is now called Gaelic. I have looked up this word in my book, and this is a suggestion I have come up with as there is no place of the name in Scotland: Nieve, which would be pronounced Newav in a Scott's accent and it means fist. Linn, a gorge through which a torrent of water falls, is pronounced leen. So there is your word newavleen.

The other statement you made about *Quote* (Better bairns greet than bearded men) was a remark made by the Master of Glammis to King James VI in that well known piece of Scottish history known as the raid of Ruthven.

Gowrie and others of the Barons having formed the generous design of freeing James VI when a youth, from his worthless favourites, inveigled him into this castle (Ruthven Castle), on his return from a hunting match in Athol. When about to depart, he was stopped by his nobles, who presented him with a memorial of their grievances. He endeavored to free himself from their restraint, and burst into tears; upon which the Master of Glammis observed, that it was better children weep than bearded men. The nobles carried him off; but he escaped, and again gave himself up to the Earl of Arran; and though he passed an act of oblivion in their favor, pronounced the conspirators guilty of high treason; and after a mock trial, perfidiously put Gowrie to death at Stirling.

On March 21, 1970, Pamela reported an unexpected "resurgence" of impressions about the Scottish girl.

The girl is having one of her "spells" again. I wanted to tell you of some names; of which I am not sure if she said or if I imagined them.

The names are: Lord Patrick, Earl William, and Earl Hom.

Also, would Saint John's stone and black pike mean anything to you? She also says of being something of honor to a queen.

Bearing in mind that I had told Pamela nothing whatever about her previous incarnation except that it had to do with Scotland, I was fascinated by this material. I contacted my good friends in Aberdeen for documentation.

Under dateline of April 14, 1970, the historian C.I.A. Ritchie, Ph.D., informed Elizabeth Byrd as follows:

> Earl William may be William Earl of Douglas, murdered by King James. Earl Hom must be Alexander Hume or Home, first Earl of Home, 1566–1619. Lord Patrick, the third Lord Gowrie, father of the Earl Gowrie. St. John's Stone is St. Johnstone, old name for Perth.

Alanna Knight and her husband checked the material out also and discovered that the ancient name for the city of Perth was St. John's Toun, and that it was two miles from Huntingtower!

From an archaeologist friend, Dr. Margaret Steward, residing in Perth, the Knights discovered that "Black Pike" may be a corruption for *Black Park*, a small estate with an old mansion house, four miles north of Huntingtower.

Not to belabor my point, but how could a 20-year-old Illinois hospital worker with only a high school education have such intimate and detailed knowledge of a very small and obscure area in Scotland . . . unless she had been there . . . *sometime.*

CHAPTER ELEVEN

The Many Lives
of a Connecticut Lady

RUTH MACGUIRE CONTACTED ME for the first time on May 10, 1967. She had read two of my books and was fascinated by her own ability to foretell future events, which she has been able to do through most of her adult life. She felt that she wanted to communicate them to me and perhaps obtain some information as to how she could develop her own mediumship in the process. I asked her to return a report to me in which she would state briefly all that she considered of an ESP nature throughout her life.

Ruth MacGuire lives in a former inn on one of Connecticut's busier highways. Separated from her husband and now divorced, Ruth lives the life of a Connecticut gypsy, not the least bit worried about tomorrow or financial problems, knowing, somehow, that everything will be all right in the end.

One sentence in her letter made me take notice, and gave me a vague feeling that this visit might be something more than a routine checkup on someone who has had psychic experiences in the past. Wondering if I had ever done any studies in the field of reincarnation, such as Edgar Cayce had done, she reported, "I have a strange memory of England in the last century which has obsessed me since childhood, and although my ancestors were English, Irish, and Danish, and I was born here, as were my parents, I find that when I'm very tired, that I always use the

English spelling as in honor, with honour and theatre. I don't do this when I'm aware of what I'm writing, but only when extremely fatigued."

How could I resist such an interesting sentence? That and the name of her place, The Old Chestnut Inn, were enough to make our trip come about earlier than I had hoped. I offered to regress her hypnotically on the occasion of my visit, and she accepted gladly.

"You mentioned some form of reincarnation memories," I began when everyone had settled down. "Can you tell me when this first started?"

"I have always remembered my early years," Ruth began, "and so it wasn't much of a surprise that I could see places at an early age that other children could not. When I was four years old, I had the very distinct impression that I knew a fourteenth-century garden somewhere in France. There wasn't much else, just the picture of the garden. Then, when I was six years old, I had the impression that I had lived in seventeenth-century Holland. It was a feeling of having lived at Leyden as a Puritan expatriate in poor health and disgusted with the robust Dutch revelings in the inn where I lived. I remember an early death. When I was seven, I had a very strange longing to dance around a Greek temple in the moonlight, wearing a flowing robe. I put this down to sheer romanticism, but for a seven-year-old this seemed to be rather a passionate longing. I have always had a longing for Greek things ever since, and the feeling for the white temple has persisted in me strongly since that time. Around the same time, I developed a strong feeling for England, and I gradually turned into an Anglophile, which I still am.

"My whole life became oriented toward England; that is to say, the England of the last century. So much so, that I was convinced that it still existed somewhere."

"Can you give me any details of these past lives?" I inquired.

"It was always as a woman," Ruth replied. "Once I drowned. I know what it is like to feel the suffocating water close over one's face and to slip down into the darkness. I also know what it is like to lie in an open coffin and to listen to comments, or to try to raise your arm, to tell onlookers that you are conscious, only to find the arm like iron, utterly immovable. The awareness of these experiences, the drowning and death, came to me in a vivid dream when I was nine.

"Now, I must admit to having a phenomenal memory, which goes back to one year of life. My aunt and my mother often used to say, 'But you can't remember that. You were only eighteen months old.' Yet I would describe a kimono my aunt wore, or the lighting fixtures in an apartment, and both turned out to be correct.

"I also have a vivid imagination, which is one reason I try to hold myself in check. There is also another strange thing: I can on occasion reach feats of accomplishment which do not have any relationship to my ordinary capabilities, almost as if I did not do these things. Once I came home from a movie, and although I play very badly, if at all, I was able to play a concerto by Max Steiner on the piano, as if I knew it."

"Another time I painted a seascape because I had to see the sea. I had never before painted in oil. I am not a painter. I have danced a Hindu folk dance, made Danish pastry, and recently acted with an amateur drama group, and have been accused of professional status in all these endeavors. No wonder I feel like an impostor."

After a moment of silence, I continued questioning her. "Have you at any time had a definite impression of being in a place where you could identify people or the names of towns or anything like that, perhaps?"

"I have very strong feelings about the year 1857 in India. I feel that that was a tremendously traumatic year for me. I have a feeling that my life ended in 1857. When I was just a child, I picked up a ten-cent piece dated 1857. As I looked at the date on the coin, I felt terribly depressed, and my body was seized with trembling. Somehow the date meant something to me."

"You mentioned memories of having lived in England, India, and Holland. Have you ever been to these places?"

"No, unfortunately not. I was born in New York City; both my parents were born in New York City, and except for a brief visit to Canada, I have never left this country."

"Have you ever had any recurrent dreams?"

"Yes, when I was a small child I often dreamt of a scene in which I saw some flat land and two women who were with me. The dream always ended in sheer panic. In the midst of the flat land there were some dark, cylindrical objects which seemed to frighten me. When I was in Canada and stood on flat land with tall buildings in the distance, there was a vague feeling of recognition, as if the tall objects were some forms of buildings, but gradually I realized that what I was seeing were windmills in the Dutch landscape, which, of course, is very flat.

"Gradually I became aware of the fact that there was a terrible sense of pressure and hurrying and trying to escape, and it tied up with another dream I had had all through my childhood, of running down steps—flights after flights of steps—with someone in pursuit. I used to wake up in terror, absolutely unable to breathe, so real was the experience. I had the distinct impression that I was running for my life. Somehow the two dreams interconnected."

"Did you see the person who was pursuing you?"

"No, I only knew there were people. I could hear the footsteps. I seemed to feel that they were some kind of guards or soldiers, but I couldn't see them. I saw swords. The atmosphere was that of the middle sixteen hundreds. Glimpses of boots on the stairs; high boots and a cloak, but not really the person. I felt it was in Holland."

"How long did this last?"

"I'd say for about ten years, and then it gradually faded away. It didn't occur any longer. The dreams were almost identical all those years. It never came back, but in the 1940s I had a terrible sense of terror again when I saw a Dutch plate with a windmill on it. Somehow it reawakened forgotten memories in me."

"Did you see yourself in these visions and dreams?" I asked.

"Yes."

"How did you look?"

"Very much the same as I look now, except that my hair was darker and I think I had brown eyes; I'm not sure. The face was very similar, the nose a bit sharper, pointed upward, and slender. I have also seen myself in another incarnation as an Englishwoman, one who died at age twenty-seven, I believe."

"Do you ever get any names?"

"No, I'm sorry. I didn't get any names, just a strong sense of identity."

"Do you ever get any feelings about locations, places?" I asked.

"I get Lucknow, in India. I have a feeling about that, but not as an Indian, rather as an Anglican living in India. I've always had a very strong pull toward India, mixed feelings of fascination and loathing at the same time."

"You mentioned the year 1857 and India before. Is there any connection between that and the memory of India and Lucknow, which you have just mentioned?" I asked.

"It could be. There is a feeling of terror, and yet a great love of Indian music, and then there is a great fear of a dark-skinned man. I don't know what it is."

"Consciously speaking, and logically, does the year 1857 mean anything to you?"

"Well, the only thing I can think of is my grandmother. She was born in 1857, but that hardly seems important."

"Have you ever had dreams where you seem to be falling from great heights?"

"Yes, something to do with the stairs. When I was being pursued, I would touch the top of a long flight of marble steps, touch it with my foot and fly and touch the bottom step with my foot, as if I were taking giant strides. I had a terrible sensation of pain in the pit of my stomach, much as one feels when the elevator misses the floor slightly and pulls up."

"Was there any continuance of the picture?"

"I just kept on going. It was as if, if I stopped, something terrible would happen to me, but I never knew quite what it was. I never stopped running."

"How did you get out after you fell down the stairs? How did you see yourself get out?"

"I didn't really fall, I just sort of touched. It was miraculous the way I took those stairs."

"How were you dressed?"

"I had a cloak and long skirt. That's all I can see—lots of petticoats and long skirts."

"What period would you say they belonged to?"

"I'd say the early 1600s, perhaps 1630 or 1640."

"During your meetings with mediums or psychics in connection with your interest in ESP, did you ever discuss your visions and dreams?"

"No, I really have never discussed it with them. Many psychics have told me that I, too, was psychic, but I didn't feel like discussing this, as I was afraid of being laughed at. I didn't want people to think I was too imaginative."

"Have you ever been hypnotized?"

"No."

"Do you think you would make a good subject?"

"I think so, because I have a very cooperative nature."

I then proceeded to suggest to her that she should relax completely and told her that I would take her back ten years at a time.

When she was ten years old (by suggestion, that is), I asked her where she lived.

"In Manhattan, 3852 Nagel Avenue."

"What is your father's name?"

"Thomas Francis Raymond."

"What is your mother's name?"

"Charlotte MacGuire."

"Where do you go to school?"

"P.S. 52."

"What is your favorite teacher's name?"

"Miss MacLoughlin."

"What does she teach you?"

"Poetry; she proclaims poetry."

"What is your homeroom teacher's name?"

"*She* was. She taught me everything. She wore black chiffon to school with beads. She said, 'I wish children would be neater. I get a very clear picture of the kind of home they come from, and I know if I went to Ruth MacGuire's home, everything would be lovely. Everything would be very neat and perfect, because that is the impression that she gives,' and I was very much chagrined, because the other children laughed."

"I then regressed her to age seven and asked her again where she lived.

"2339 Davidson Avenue in the Bronx."

"Where do you go to school?"

"St. Nicholas of Tolentine Parochial School."

"What is your favorite teacher's name?"

"She was a nun, Sister Bonaventura."

I proceeded to take her back further, year by year. Then I crossed the threshold of birth and suggested that she go back to minus five, minus ten, minus twenty years.

"What do you see now? Look around."

"It's all vapors, big thick clouds and vapors, and it's cold, very cold."

"I suggested she go back even further and told her to go back to one hundred years before her birth.

"Where are you now?"

"I'm in England—Sussex,"

"Where in Sussex?"

"I don't know yet—wait, there is a house and a lawn and my sister."

"What is your sister's name?"

"Ann."

"What is your name?"

"Martha."

"What is your father's name?"

"George."

"What is the family name, his entire name?"

"Andrews."

"What does he do?"

"A lawyer."

"Where does he live? What town?"

"Buck . . . Buck . . . no, Stokeley. Something to do with Stokeley and Buckminster. I don't know, He's not here all the time. He goes away."

"Where is the house?"

"It's in the country, but he has to go to the city sometimes."

"What town is the house in?"

"Two names—Stokeley on Bow . . . no."

"What county is it in?"

"Stokeley on Bow in Sussex . . . something like that."

Later I checked up on these places. It was most unlikely for Ruth MacGuire to have any intimate knowledge of villages and obscure little towns in England, having never gone there nor having studied English geography to any extent. There is no Stokeley in England. However, I found a Stockesley in Yorkshire. There is also a Stockesby, and as for Buckminster, it does exist. Buckminster is on the border between Leicestershire and Lincolnshire, and as I looked at a detailed map of the area, I discovered that very close to Buckminster there are two other villages that might conceivably be the "Stokeley" the entranced Ruth MacGuire was talking about. There is a Stonesby west of Buckminster and there is a

Stokerochford north of Buckminster. Both of these villages are very close to Buckminster. As for the word *Bow*, there is a village named Bow in Cornwall, but I doubt that there is any connection between Cornwall and Yorkshire in this instance. There is no Stokeley on Bow in Sussex. In fact, none of the places here mentioned are in Sussex, which is much farther south. Why the entranced subject confused the counties, I do not know, but I find it rather remarkable that she came up with the name Buckminster, a village or small town of which I have never heard and which I found only by consulting the detailed map of British counties I have in my possession. Meanwhile, I continued my questioning.

"What year are we in now?"

"1809."

"What is your mother's name?"

"My mother isn't there. She is dead."

I insisted on her mother's name.

"Mabel."

"What was she before she married your father?"

"Mabel Breen."

"When did she die?"

"She died when I was two years old, in 1800, I think."

"Where did you go to school?"

"I didn't."

"Where did you go to church?"

"The Parish Church . . . Saint something. I didn't like the minister."

"What was his name, and what was the name of the church?"

"He had two names, Holly Benton, and he spit when he preached."

"Do you remember the name of the church?

"Yes, St. Hildegard."

"Where was it located?"

"In the village. We walked, and I had such a pretty hat."

"Where was your house?"

"Just outside the village. Oh, it was a pretty little house. It had dormer windows. It was of stone . . . no, brick, and big, wide windows and a green lawn, and such lovely roses in the garden, and they took very good care of the garden of Mrs. Benton . . . Mrs. Benton was the housekeeper."

"Did you live there or did you leave town?" I asked.

"I lived there until I got married."

"Whom did you marry?"

"An officer in the service."

"What was his name?"

"Ronald Whiting."

"What branch of the service was he in?"

"Her Majesty's Troops Dragoons. I hated it."

"Do you remember what number the regiment was?"

"Number 67, I think."

"Who was the colonel of the regiment? Do you remember the commanding officer's name?"

"Oh, him. I didn't like him at all."

"But, what was his name?"

"Edgeworth."

"Do you remember any other officers in the regiment?"

"No, I wasn't very well, and I went sometimes to the regimental affairs, but I didn't like them very much. I hated the military."

"After you were married, where did you go to live?"

"I always dreaded being sent away . . . sent to places so far away."

"What do you mean, 'so far away'? Where were you sent?"

"We went to India."

"Where in India?"

"Calcutta, and then another place where there was an uprising."

"Where was the uprising? Was it a town, a fort?"

"Not a big city like Calcutta. I think it was a town—Mysore, if there is such a place."

When I nodded that there was indeed such a place, she continued.

"My husband was very angry because I didn't like that kind of living . . . always on the move. I wanted to go back to England. It was so hot. Sometimes it was so dirty, and the natives distressed me while they fascinated me, and I couldn't cope with the whole problem in India. I wanted to do something about it and I couldn't. I just fumed and fretted. I felt it was all wrong. I couldn't see why we had to be there, and then he would go away. He would always go away leaving me with the servants. There were plenty of servants. There was nothing for me to do, of course."

"Was that in Mysore?"

"Both in Calcutta and Mysore and then this other place."

She seemed to have trouble remembering the other place, so I asked, "What year are we now?"

"Eighteen-fifty-two we went there. We had to stay there for five years before we could be sent anywhere else, and there was this terrible day when he wasn't there. He had gone away."

"Where had he gone to?"

"Oh, he had to go away. They had to go away. They thought trouble was coming."

"Who was making trouble? Who were the people that were making the trouble?"

"The natives were very angry. They didn't want us there."

"Were these the native Indians?"

"Yes."

"Were they civilians?"

"Oh, they were civilians, and there were some army Sikhs and they came in one day like a dam breaking . . . came in, the bodies screaming, shouting, pillaging, raping. I ran and hid. The children, they got it, it was terrible . . . all the bloodshed and the wickedness, and there was no place to run . . . nowhere. I was so soiled . . . so deeply crushed. They spared nobody. They were frenzied, wild, with bloodshot eyes, angry, rioting."

"What year was that in?"

"We went to India in 1852, and we stayed there five years."

"It was 1857, then?"

"Yes."

"And what happened after that? Did you leave India?"

"Well, yes, we did. I had to leave, but it was the end of everything for me. Well, I wasn't killed. It would have been better if I had been."

"What about your husband?"

"He wasn't there. He had been sent on this other foolish chase. They thought trouble was coming."

"Where from?"

"The other end. The other end, two miles away, and then they came and nothing was sacred, absolutely nothing . . . the children killed and wounded, stomped upon."

"Where was that?"

"In Lucknow. Yes, in Lucknow, at the officers' quarters. It

was terrible, and this Indian came. He was very tall, very menacing, very dark. I thought he was going to strangle me, but he raped
me. Isn't that awful? I never knew why there had to be an empire.
Just that little green island would have been enough. Why did we
have to go out there in the first place?"

"Where was your husband at the time?"

"He had been sent with the troops to the other end, where
they had suspected there would be trouble, and while they were
gone, the men came, wild, a flood of human hatred, and, oh, there
was no appeal. There was nothing that could reach them. This
large menacing man, with a large aquiline nose, pinned me to the
wall. He had a stare, and I hoped that he was going to kiss me, but
he didn't. He was disgusting, fascinating, but it was awful, because
some of us didn't die. We have to live with that memory."

"You went back to England then?"

"I never got there."

"What happened to you?"

"I fell."

"Where did you fall?"

"On the ship. I don't know whether I fell or whether I was
pushed. I was so unhappy."

"Where did the ship go to?"

"It was going back to England. My husband was furious."

"Why was he furious?"

"He was very unreasonable. I think that he wished that I had
been killed instead of raped. He said I was . . . well, having been
touched by a native, was unclean. He wouldn't even talk to me."

"And when you fell on the ship, what happened then to you?"

"I drowned. I could feel the water closing over my face, and I
didn't care, and it was frightening. For a moment I struggled, and
then a strange feeling of happiness came over me. I had tried to
breathe, but I couldn't, and so I gave up the struggle."

"What was the next thing that happened to you then?"

"I fainted. I just breathed in the water, and I don't remember
anything. Yes, I remember being dead. They must have got my
body. I remember being in a coffin. They must have retrieved it,
because it was in a coffin, and they were making the kind of remarks that people do."

"Did you see yourself in the coffin?"

"Yes. I must have been on shipboard. I saw the coffin and the people passing by, and I wanted to tell them, 'I hear what you are saying. I hear,' and I tried to move my arm. I tried, and it was like lead. I couldn't move. I couldn't wiggle. I couldn't even move my nose . . . couldn't even indicate that I was there and I was listening."

"And after that?"

"Nothing after that . . . nothing."

Later I researched this amazing account of her presence in another lifetime during the Indian rebellion. To begin with, Ruth MacGuire is not a student of Indian history. If she had any general knowledge of British Imperial policies in India during the nineteenth century, it would not include specifics as to where battles and sieges took place. But I questioned Ruth thoroughly, and I am convinced that she did not even have that much knowledge about British India during the time of Queen Victoria, nor did she, indeed, show any interest in this period, except for what happened to her in another life.

If Ronald Whiting was a member of the 67th Dragoons, he could have been in British India at the critical moment. The rebellion took place in 1857. The Sikhs did indeed play a role in it, although at various times they supported the British colonial effort and not always that of the rebels.

A little later, I asked the entranced Ruth to go back into her Indian past and to answer a few questions.

"What is a *sepoy?*"

Without a moment's hesitation, she answered, "A sepoy . . . it's a kind of a native."

"What does he do? What does a sepoy do professionally?"

"He's with the troops, isn't he?"

I very much doubt Ruth MacGuire would have had the knowledge to describe correctly the meaning of the word *sepoy*. The fact that she did not use this term does not mean that she did not know it. I deliberately tried it on her to see what her reaction would be.

She spoke of Lucknow and the terrible things that happened there. It is a historical fact that the compound at Lucknow was under siege by the rebel troops, and that thousands were actually killed during that period both at Lucknow and at Delhi. Delhi had been in the hands of the rebels but was finally besieged and taken back by the British colonial troops, at which time a great bloodbath took place. Lucknow was then free, and the women and children and the remnants of the garrison left. It is also true that many, if not most, of the women were shipped home to England after their two years of terror during the rebellion in India.

Since Ruth had spoken of other incarnations when we discussed her memories in the conscious state, I decided to take her back even further. I commanded her to go back beyond India, and to go further back in time.

"It is now three hundred years before your present birth. What do you see?" I asked.

"Smoke in the room. A fireplace. I am in a room in a cottage, and the fireplace is smoking. It burns my throat, and they can't open the window. It's cold, and they won't open the door."

"Do you see yourself?"

"Yes."

"How old do you look?"

"About twelve."

"Do you know your name?"

"It's a Biblical name . . . Magdalene . . . Magdalene Darling."

"In what town are you?"

"Now we are in Holland. We are not in England but we speak English, and the other people don't."

"What is the year?"

"The year is 1613."

"And what is the town?"

"Leyden."

"Why are you here?"

"Everything gets sort of stupid. My father was there but he wasn't around very much, and my aunt and my mother are both there, and we have to wait and, and there is something about the new world, in passage."

"On what ship is the passage?"

"We don't know. We are waiting and we have rooms at the inn—this inn in the town."

"Who is sending the ships?"

"Well, you see, we are not very well thought of in England, I am sorry to say. We are very respectable people, really. Perhaps too respectable.

"What faith are you?"

"Oh, we are Puritans."

"Do you remember the name of the company who sends the ships . . . the name of the owner of the ships?"

Well, I didn't pay very much attention to things like that. I wasn't well, you see. I had this cough. My mother and my aunt—they were there. They hated it, and they kept saying that I had to have good courage, strong faith, or, We'd come to the new world . . . everything would be different. We wouldn't have to be persecuted and all that, but it seemed so hopeless. We were there so long."

"What town did your people come from in England?"

"My father comes from the North."

"What town does he come from?"

"North Riding on the Moors."

"Where in the North Riding? What village?"

"Horton."

"What is your father's name?"

"John Darling."

"And your mother's name?"

"My mother was Johanna."

"And what was her maiden name before her marriage?"

"Bliss."

"Where did she come from? What town in England?"

"She, too, came from the North . . . Durham. It's near Newcastle somewhere."

Again, my later research established the validity of Ruth's statement. Horton is indeed in Yorkshire, although on present-day maps it is in the West Riding rather than in the North Riding, but it is in the northern part of the West Riding, as this particular area is even now called. Durham is indeed directly south of Newcastle and also not very far from Horton. Only someone very familiar with English geography would have such knowledge. I have been in the area, and I do not recall these places. The name Darling, incidentally, is quite common in Yorkshire.

In 1612 the Dutch founded New Amsterdam, which is now New York City. Actually, the Puritans who had come to Holland because of persecutions at home in England emigrated a few years later than the date of 1613 given by Ruth in trance. Most of the emigrés left between 1629 and 1637, but it is entirely possible that some left at an earlier date. There is no doubt that English Puritans did spend time in Holland, which was much more favorably inclined toward their religion. Leyden is the nearest large city toward the coast opposite England. Many Puritans did, indeed, find refuge in seventeenth-century Leyden.

I continued to question Ruth.

"Now you are going with them to the New World?"

"Yes, my aunt, my mother's sister, we are supposed to go to the Plymouth Colony, but are we ever going to get there? There is never any room on the ships. We have to wait and wait, and disaster after disaster, and mother said I'd end up speaking Dutch, which she didn't particularly want. She said they were . . . oh, she used a word that expressed contempt . . . blubbers. She said they were bear blubbers; but you see, it was at the inn, and these men were quite coarse. Mother was not, of course."

"Do you remember the name of the inn in Leyden?"

"Three Turks, I think."

"And the year is still 1613?"

"Yes, and it's damp and cold, but the fire is always smoking, and then, of course, it's always brighter and warmer downstairs, but we don't want to go down there because those roistering Dutchmen . . . well, my mother doesn't want me to be exposed to them."

"Did you take the ship across?"

"No, I never got there. I died in Leyden."

"How old were you then?"

"Thirteen."

"And you parents returned to England?"

"I don't know what happened to them, really, I had this cough, and it was miserable, and I was in bed. I couldn't leave the room, and they kept saying, 'Courage, child. You'll get well,' but I . . ."

"How long did you stay in Holland?"

"Three years."

"Did you always live in the inn?"

"Well, we lived with a family at first, but it was rather crowded, and my father said we were best off at the inn."

"What sort of place did the family have?"

"It was a farm out in the country, and I liked that much better because there were apple trees and the cows and windmills, and it was fun to watch them going around."

"Did you like the windmills?"

"Yes, I liked them in the daytime. I loved to watch them, but at night they sort of frightened me because they looked so like giants with seven arms going around and around, waiting to devour. The children were nice, and the Dutch people were nice on the farm, but when we had to go into town, it was different."

"What was the name of the farm in the little village you lived in? Do you remember that?"

"Greck, or something."

"Was it near Leyden?"

"Leyden was the nearest big city to it."

"What province was that in?"

"It began with a U . . . U . . . "

"Was it Utrecht?"

"Yes, that was it—Utrecht, but we didn't pay much attention to where we were then. We were glad to get out of England, and there were lots of things to do—ice skating in the winter, an iceboat, and I loved that, but then when we went to the city it was horrid and not very clean, and then I died in the inn, in the room at the inn."

The hour was growing late. I detected signs of weariness in Ruth and decided to bring her back into the present.

In February of 1968 she communicated with me again. She vividly described a market place in Calcutta and then added some details to her frightful experience of going back to England aboard ship. Apparently, she had become pregnant as a result of the experience that she had gone through during the siege of Lucknow. In addition, she had formed some sort of attachment to an Indian officer aboard ship, who had first protected her from the others and then forced his attentions upon her in private. Despite the strong impression, in her own mind she still doubted the validity of these prenatal experiences and made it a point to warn me that she could not prove any of it.

We communicated and corresponded off and on and met a couple of times for dinner. These occasions were always delightful and festive, but we did not discuss the serious business of reincarnation at such times. Evidently, the visions remained in her subconscious mind, and in some instances became deeper, for in July of 1969 she jotted down some of the most important ones for me.

The vision of a market place in Calcutta was even more vivid now. The colonel's wife is named Dora, and she is in the market to look at brassware, pottery, fabric, and food. Dora wears a green-and-white plaid dress with a flounced skirt, while Ruth wears a pale straight muslin. Both women wear bonnets and carry sunshades. A woman squats near a low table on which are arranged some sweets made from apricots. She is nursing an infant whose head is covered with flies. Dora takes a handkerchief from her bag and gives it to the woman, indicating that she is to wave off the flies with it. The woman smiles her thanks and places the handkerchief on the baby's head. The two women move on.

A second vision concerns a stone church in England with a square tower covered with ivy. Ruth sees herself standing on the steps with her new husband. He is in uniform, while she is wearing a bridal gown and veil and is very nervous. There are friends and villagers at the bottom of the path throwing petals at them. Ruth is embarrassed by this. She wishes they were on the steamer that is to take them to Calcutta. She closes her eyes and knows that she will have to walk through the crowd to get to the carriage, and she dreads it.

The third vision sees her in the compound in Lucknow. All the men have gone except for a few who are doing guard duty. The drums have been going for hours, and some of the women are beside themselves with fear but are trying not to show it. Mrs. Jennings' ayah is about to give birth. Dora is bustling about, preparing for the event. She has commandeered linens from all sources and has unguents and jars in readiness. Someone is burning incense. The ayah's moment has come. Ruth is standing by with a basin of water. She cannot stand the sights and smells, and everything turns dark green and she faints dead away.

The final vision sees her aboard ship, going home to England, but it is not a happy time. She sees herself in the bunk, with the ship pitching and tossing. She is very ill. Dora, however, thinks it is merely seasickness. She is trying to feed her gruel and tea. However, Ruth is sick for another reason. She is pregnant by the sepoy who ravished her. She is defiled. Her husband said so.

There is nothing for her to do but turn her face to the wall and die. He said so. When everyone is sleeping, she will go out on deck. She will lean over, who will care? There is nothing but disgrace, and she would be done with this life.

Now, these four visions are, in fact, only repetitions and embellishments of the material Ruth has spoken of consciously in part and more elaborately under hypnosis, but there are some details not found in the earlier versions. It is, of course, entirely possible that Ruth has embroidered her stories, either consciously or unconsciously, with details that would make them better stories, but I do not think so. She has nothing to gain from this. It is rather an unsavory experience that she is recording, and a less truthful person than Ruth might, in fact, suppress it or certain of the details. Apparently, in telling me all her reincarnation memories, Ruth has also relieved herself of the pressures that came with them. She has, I think, accepted these experiences as a legitimate part of her character and acknowledges the need for her earlier sufferings.

CHAPTER TWELVE

The Reincarnation
of an Atlanta Belle

JUNE VOLPE WAS BORN in a small town in Pennsylvania, the daughter of an average couple who now live in retirement in Florida. When she was only a teenager, June married Sam Volpe, a man of Italian extraction. She, herself, was of Dutch–German background. Eventually, they moved into a small town in western Pennsylvania, where they bought a house and where Sam followed a career in the glass industry. His work was neither extraordinary nor dull, and June's family was no different from her neighbors'.

With four children, her life was always busy, and even when the two older children left home, there was plenty to do around the house. The elder son was in the service, and one daughter was married. Only the two younger children still lived at home with June and Sam. They lived a pleasant if somewhat uneventful life, far from the mainstream of adventure, far from any big city. To reach Pittsburgh, the nearest big city, requires many hours of driving.

June has been to Long Island and knows some parts of New York State in addition to her own Pennsylvania, but it wasn't until 1959, when she was twenty-nine years old, that June went on her first major trip. In June of that year she undertook her first visit south, to Florida, where her parents then lived.

The first week of her stay in Silver Springs passed uneventfully. It had been raining, and June was somewhat concerned about the lack of good weather. One evening she found herself sitting in the kitchen mending some clothes when her older daughter, who was then living with June's parents, came up to her and said, "Mamma, before you go home, I want you to come and see the haunted house."

June started to laugh, for the very notion of a haunted house was totally alien to her. She just didn't believe in such things, but her daughter insisted.

"No, really, Mamma. They say it's haunted by the lady who used to live there."

June is a practical-minded person, and she was about to dismiss the remark of her fifteen-year-old daughter when her mother spoke up, suggesting that she go over to the site next morning right after breakfast. June, wanting to end the conversation, agreed half-heartedly to go and have a look at this haunted house. With that, the subject was dropped, and the conversation turned to family matters.

Around eleven-thirty, June went to bed and quickly dropped off to sleep. Suddenly, she found herself in a two-seated wagon with a fringed top. Two men sat in front talking and a large colored woman was at her side, grumbling to herself, seemingly quite concerned for June's welfare. The strange thing was that June saw *herself* wearing a long, full, ruffled white dress. Her hair was long, auburn in color. In her hand she held a parasol, which she was moving around with nervous gestures. She wanted to hurry, to go faster, and she felt excitement racing through her body as she pleaded with the driver to go faster.

They drove now through a small town and over a dirt road, past wooden frame and brick homes, shops, and a church—all of them with metal hitching posts, most of black iron with a horse's head or an angel on top and a metal ring to tie the horses to. Next she saw a little red railroad station and narrow-gauge track, and a pretty fountain with three cherubs blowing little horns, with the water streaming out of them. The streets were lined with palms and large shade trees dripping with moss. A warm, pleasant breeze blew, ruffling her skirt and hair, which was hanging long about her shoulders. Now the carriage reached the end of town and went down a dirt road to her left. On one side she noticed tall golden wheat swaying in the soft breeze. On the other side of the road there was tall corn. The young man driving the two-horse carriage turned and shouted to her, "There it is. You can see it from here."

"Where, where? Oh, yes, I can see it. Please, hurry. Hurry, or I shall get out and run to it by myself."

The man laughed in a teasing way and hurried the horses on a bit faster to the curve at the end of the lane.

A large white two-story house stood there, with a circular drive and a large shade tree in front of the porch, which extended across the front of the house. Flowers grew about the yard, and the lawn was a green carpet, spread out as if just for her. The carriage had barely stopped when she stepped down and went up onto the porch and through the front door, into a large hallway. She heard herself screaming with delight as she raced from one room to the next.

"Oh, it's beautiful and I love it, and it's mine, all mine," she heard herself say. She noticed a stairway going up to the right. At the foot of the staircase was a room toward the left. Then, coming through the front door, to the right she noticed a library. A painted mural of a hunting scene was on the left-hand wall, above a red velvet love seat decorated in the Victorian manner. Bookshelves, reaching from floor to ceiling against the wall, were separated by a lovely wood and brick fireplace. The walls were all white throughout the house.

She found herself walking through the house looking at all the rooms, noticing that there were five bedrooms upstairs, and noticing that each of them had a fireplace and that they were furnished beautifully. An overwhelming feeling of having come home pervaded her, and she was very happy and filled to the brim with contentment.

In the dream, she saw herself, yet not looking like herself, but somehow feeling identical with the person going through the house. The girl she saw looked to be about eighteen or nineteen years old, possibly a few years older, and not at all like the person June was at the time of her dream. Still, she could not understand how she could be both her present self and also the girl in the dream.

She awoke early with a strange, eerie, almost sickening, feeling. She couldn't understand this, for it had been a lovely dream. Why would it make her feel so bad? The more she tried to shake off the vivid memory of the dream and the strange, unsettled feeling that came with it, the worse she began to feel.

The rain had stopped now, and it was a warm, humid morning. As soon as breakfast and the dishes were finished, June's father reminded her that she had promised to go and have a look at the haunted house. Still under the unsettling influence of her dream, June reluctantly agreed. Her daughter Lolly and her son Mich came along for the ride. Evidently, her father noticed that she wasn't quite herself. "What's the matter with you this morning, June?" he inquired. She only shook her head. "It's nothing. I just had a bad dream. I'll be all right." Her father nodded and let the matter rest.

After awhile the scene seemed strangely familiar. With mounting excitement, she noticed that she knew the way, yet she also knew that she had never been here before in her life. Soon the car entered a totally deserted "ghost town" called Red Mill. The town was exactly the same as she had seen it in the dream the night before, but now the houses and shops were all crumbling; even the fountain in the middle of town was in shambles. June knew every part of the place. She knew where her father would have to turn off to get into the lane leading to the house of her dream, and before she knew it, that was exactly what he was doing. It was all very frightening and confusing, yet the excitement was as strong as it had been in her dream.

Her father stopped the car at the entrance to an overgrown lane. The wheat and corn fields of her dream were gone now, and only weeds, tall grass, and underbrush grew. The house was black with age and falling down. The porch was all but gone. Suddenly, she found herself racing as fast as she could toward the house, with the children in close pursuit. Her father had declined to come along, as he had some business to take care of in town. He would be back for them later. Her daughter had been to the house many times before without experiencing anything special. To her, it was just an old house, perhaps with eerie overtones, and fun to play in, but there were no actual psychic overtones, nor was there anything out of the ordinary surrounding the old, broken-down house.

The house was quite empty now, except for some grain that was being stored in the living room by a rental farmer, but June did not see the house as it was now. Rather did she experience it, somehow, as it had been when she had known it in another lifetime. She felt a surge of happy contentment, as if she had been away for a long, long time and had finally returned home.

Room by room, June and her two children went through the house now. She remembered how the lace curtains moved gently over the dining room windows, but, of course, that was impossible. There were no lace curtains anymore. Everything was gone except the faded-out hunting scene painted on the library wall. It was the same scene she had seen in her dream the night before.

"There used to be a desk over there," June heard herself mumble. "And the settee went over there."

"Mamma, how do you know?" her daughter said, somewhat frightened by her mother's strange knowledge of a house she had never seen in her life before.

June did not answer. She wondered about it herself.

On the way over, Lolly had told her mother about a terrible murder that had taken place in this very house. This was the first time that June had heard about Mrs. Simms. Apparently, her daughter had picked up some of the local stories concerning the abandoned house. A Mrs. Elizabeth Simms had once lived in it and had been murdered, but the cause of her death and the name of her murderer had never been discovered.

Now June stood in the house that she knew so well and yet couldn't really know. She followed her children up the stairs and heard her daughter say, "Mamma, this is the room that Mrs. Simms was murdered in." Despite the grim words, June felt peaceful in that room. After awhile she descended the stairs and returned to the library.

Outside, a thundershower was coming down, and they decided to wait until it stopped. By this time, June's father would have returned and was probably waiting outside at the end of the lane. While they were waiting, Lolly suddenly said, "I wonder what the last thing was she did before she went upstairs and was murdered that night."

No sooner had her daughter said this than June felt unseen hands clutch her waist from behind, and she seemed to have no control over her body at all or even over what she was saying. Somehow she was moved first to the fireplace.

"She stood here for a moment, looking at the pictures on the mantel," she heard herself say in a very strange voice. Next she was literally moved across the room, through the doorway, and up the stairs. "She held the candle with one hand and held up her skirt hem with the other. She was very tired and worried about something."

June could hear her daughter say, pleadingly, "Mamma, what's the matter? You look funny, Mamma. You're so white. You're frightening me, Mamma. Don't do that. What's the matter?" But June couldn't really hear her. She couldn't speak. When she reached the second step from the top, she heard loud footsteps hurrying down the hall, coming close to her. Suddenly, she panicked and turned. She could not move down the stairs. Something was pushing her back, wanting her to go on up. Desperately, June grabbed onto the railing and, hand over hand, pulled herself to the bottom of the staircase. Her new blouse was ripped up the back. She felt sick to her stomach and stood on the front porch, or what was still left of the porch, for awhile, breathing deeply and with difficulty the fresh, cool air. Her panic was gone now, and she could vividly remember the impression of human hands on her back. No doubt about it, someone in the house, unseen though that person might have been, wanted her to go up the stairs.

June and her children started to leave, but she kept hearing someone calling to her from the house, "Come back. Please come back. Don't go, please." Desperately she fought a battle within herself not to turn and run back to the house and up those stairs. Finally, she turned to look back, and when she did, she saw a young girl in a long white dress, with long brown hair, standing at the window. The girl in the window looked a lot like her.

In the car on their way back to Silver Springs, the children asked why she had behaved in such a strange manner. "You frightened us, Mamma," her daughter said. June nodded grimly. She was frightened herself. Neither of her children had heard the voice nor seen the apparition at the window, but they had seen her behavior on the stairs and noticed the tearing of her blouse.

That evening she mentioned her experience to her parents. "Well, these things do happen," her father had said, and with this remark, the matter was dropped.

As the days went on, June became more and more convinced that the apparition at the window had been merely her exaggerated imagination. For some reason, she thought, she had become agitated, and in the nervous state she was in, due to the strange experience on the stairs, she might have imagined seeing a woman where there was in reality no one.

During the rest of her stay in Silver Springs, she had no further unusual dreams. When she returned home to Pennsylvania a month later, however, her husband noticed a great change in her. It was almost as if she had become another person. Where her temperament before her trip to Florida had been rather timid and complacent, she now seemed to be much more demanding and sophisticated in her interests. There was a lively enthusiasm, a desire to fight for what she believed in, that had not existed before.

Ever since her strange experience at the crumbling house, she had a strong desire to return, and she knew that she would have to go back there someday. From time to time she noticed a southern accent in her speech. The whole incident left her no peace, and eventually she wrote to her father and asked for his help to find out once and for all what it all meant. Her father suggested that she get in touch with an old gentleman who had been the postmaster when Red Mill was still a going town. He might be a good source of information about the Simms family and that which transpired about a hundred years ago.

After several letters, June finally received an answer. Yes, there had been a Simms family, with seven children, and there was a lot of heartache in that family. There was, first of all, Laura Lee, who had run off and disappeared, and then there was Robert, who was a cripple because he had been run over by a horse and wagon.

When the place at Red Mill was still a thriving plantation, it was one of the best in the area. Apparently, Mr. and Mrs. Simms had married young. They had come from an aristocratic family in Atlanta, Georgia. They arrived in Florida around 1860, just when Florida was beginning to develop.

Allen, the oldest boy, joined the Union forces when the Civil War broke out, despite his father's protests, and was immediately disowned. He was killed in Atlanta, Georgia, trying to protect his grandparents from being killed when the Union troops moved onto their plantation. The plantation itself was burned, looted, and destroyed.

Another son served in the Confederate Army at the dispatcher's headquarters. After Robert died in an accident in the swamps, the mother was left alone, for Robert the elder had died of a stroke due to the sudden death of Allen, his favorite son.

When the war was over, Mrs. Simms decided to open a small store, not so much for financial gain as to keep herself busy. It was a grocery and supply store. At the time June had visited the house for the first and only time, she had found some yellow ledgers and notebooks in the house. They pertained mainly to the running of the grocery store. She had picked them up and kept them in her possession. There were also some letters, and it appeared from them that there was another son, James.

Mrs. Simms was eighty-nine at the time of her death. Apparently, she was brushing her hair in the bedroom when she was shot in the back with a shotgun and killed instantly. The story goes, according to the former postmaster, that James had become a traitor to the Southern cause toward the end of the war. Having gambled heavily, he was in great need of funds. For that reason, he worked with Union spies, selling them Southern secrets, but the Confederate espionage apparatus got wind of it and he escaped by the skin of his teeth. James then became a fugitive, always careful of Confederate agents. Even after the war, James was afraid for his life. No one knows whether James's mother was killed for some sort of revenge or by mistake, but the killer was never found. Apparently, the tragedy happened in 1896. The ledger, which June had discovered in the house, gave entries all the way up to 1913, so it is probable that the son still lived at that date.

A year ago her father informed June that he had heard that the place had been torn down, that there was nothing left to remind her of the once-proud plantation. Despite this, June's longing for the place was as strong as ever. In her mind's eye she would see it as it was, and she could hardly resist the desire to return to "her old home."

In addition to the house, she saw another scene time and again, a creek with lots of stones and water ripples around it, and on one side a big tree with Spanish moss hanging down from it, touching the water. The scene was peaceful and quiet, but she had never been to such a place, nor had she ever seen a similar picture.

As if her strange experiences, her change of personality, and her overwhelming desire to return to a place she hardly knew weren't enough to upset June, there was something else.

Gradually, she had become aware of another experience

somewhere in the dim, dark past of her existence. This was a memory of a girl with soft brown hair who looked a lot like her. This girl arrived home with three other women, two older ones and one her own age. They were traveling in a buggy of sorts, drawn by two horses. The driver wore a black suit, and something told her that this happened about 1693.

As the scene unrolled, she saw them stop in front of a long brick building, and felt instinctively that this was not in America but in Germany. She noticed that the girl pulled back the curtain and stepped down from the buggy, and that she was followed into the house by the others. The girl was about twenty years old, of slender build, and wearing a long, dark hooded coat wrapped tightly about her.

June felt that they had returned home from visiting a Dutch relative. The relative lived in a wooden-shingled house of two stories, with a water wheel connected with it. There was a quiet red-faced heavily built man sitting in front of the mill, and June seemed to hear some conversation in a language she thought was Dutch. Then June suddenly felt that it was she entering the kitchen of the house. A large heavily built woman who was fussing in the kitchen welcomed her. That night she slept in a large straw-filled "swinging" bed on the second floor. There were three people to a bed because it was warmer that way, and the beds were very wide.

Since June is of German-Dutch descent, she assumed that this scene had something to do with her ancestry. She did understand some Dutch and German, although she could not speak either. Still, the memory was more than just a fading scene from the past. It was something that was also very strong, though not as compelling as the identification with the unhappy woman in the Florida plantation house.

Her memories of what appear to be previous lifetimes were not like some of the ordinary memories of things she did in her past. Somehow, they were much more vivid, and they disturbed June. At one point she decided to discuss the matter with her priest. The good father listened patiently and seriously, and when June asked him whether he thought there was something wrong with her, he shook his head. "No," he said. "There is nothing wrong with you, my dear, except perhaps that you are too sensitive for your own good," and with that, he dismissed her. But June was not satisfied with such bland advice. She went to a clinic in Ridgeway, Pennsylvania, and subjected herself to every conceivable psychiatric test. Dr. John Dickerson, the resident psychiatrist, eventually sent her home with the remark that she was probably mentally healthier than he was, and that there was nothing wrong with her at all.

Since June had always rejected the possibility of the supernatural, it disturbed her to have dreamed of the Simms home before she had ever laid eyes upon it. The memory of the girl in the carriage in Germany had actually been with her for a long time before the visit to Florida. But she had never paid it any heed. Now, however, in the light of the Florida adventure, it took on new dimensions.

All these matters were on her mind when she turned on her television set one fine morning and watched me discuss psychic phenomena with Marie Torre on Pittsburgh television. All of a sudden she knew whom she could ask about her strange memories. When she contacted me, I immediately wrote back, asking her to come to meet me the next time I was in Pittsburgh.

Unfortunately, however, June was not allowed to travel much. One valve of her heart is completely blocked. She therefore doesn't travel much and must avoid strain. Her town is over one hundred miles from Pittsburgh. Regretfully, June declined to meet me, and instead issued an invitation to come and meet her at her home. Then some doubts arose in my mind. If she had such a heart defect, could I safely hypnotize her? I asked her to check the entire matter with her physician before I went any further. Then, too, I wanted her to ask her husband whether he had any objections to my starting to work with June, since it might entail a considerable amount of time and research.

If her reincarnation memories proved to be evidential, I felt that we might have to continue for a considerable length of time with hypnosis, and I wanted to make sure I would not be interrupted halfway to my goal.

On March 20, 1968, I received a most cordial letter from June. Both her personal physician and the doctor at the clinic had encouraged her to proceed with the experiment. I was told only to avoid fatiguing her, and this I readily agreed to. Her husband, Sam, also put nothing in our way, so I made arrangements for June to meet me in Pittsburgh on the first of May. Despite my offer to have her flown in from her little town in western Pennsylvania, she came by bus, and was none the worse for it.

Even our first meeting in person was rather strange. My plane had been delayed, and I had begun to worry that Mrs. Volpe might find waiting uncomfortable. Mentally, perhaps, I may have sent out some thoughts that reached her mind. After all, she had had ESP all through her life. When I reached the hotel at which she was staying, I picked up the house phone and asked for her room. At that precise moment she stepped up from behind me. She had been in her room and had suddenly gotten an intuition to go down to the lobby to greet me. Thus we met and returned immediately upstairs to begin our first hypnosis session as soon as possible.

After I had put her under, I suggested that she was getting younger. Physically her face slackened, and when I suggested that she was just six years old, you could almost see the little girl. Then she became a baby before my eyes, and finally I sent her back across the threshold of birth and suggested that the time now was fifty years before her birth as June. Another personality now seemed to possess her body.

I asked quietly, "What is your name?"

"Mary Elizabeth."

"Where do you live?"

"I live in Georgia."

"What is your mother's name?"

"Catherine."

"What is your father's name?"

"Frank."

"Where do you live in Georgia?"

"On our plantation."

"What is it called? What town is it in?"

"Atlanta—Atlanta, Georgia."

"And what's your family's name?"

"Tibbits."

"Do you have any brothers and sisters?"

"I have a brother."

"What's his name?"

"Melvin."

"How old is he?"

"Twenty-three."

"How old are you?"

"I'm eighteen."

"Where were you born?"

"Right here."

"In Atlanta?"

"Ahuh, in that little room up there at the top of the stairs."

"Where's the house? What street is the house on? The plantation, where is it? In Atlanta?"

"We have one of the largest plantations here in Atlanta, Georgia, that you'd ever want to see."

"Where did you go to school?"

"We had private tutors come in—taught my brother and I, in the library."

"What church did you go to?"

"White Baptist Church."

"Where is it located?"

"Down the lane."

"What's your grandfather's name?"

"He's dead."

"What was his name?"

"Gordon."

"Does your father serve in the Army?"

"No, Pop's too old."

"Does he have a brother in the Army?"

"No, they keep talking all the time about the Army and carpetbaggers and high taxes."

"What year is this now?"

"It's 18 . . . 18 . . . I don't know."

"What's the president's name?"

"Jackson."

"Tell me a little bit about yourself. What do you do all day?"

"Go to teas."

"Do you have any friends?"

"Robert."

"Robert what?"

"Simms."

"How old is he?"

"Twenty-two."

"What does he do? Where does he live?"

"His family lives the next plantation over."

"How far away?"

"Across the creek. Over the lane."

"Are you going to marry him?"

"Oh, yes, if I could only get him to tell me he wants to marry me. I know he wants to marry me. I don't know . . . he doesn't want to get married yet."

"Why, is he too young?"

"No, something about new land."

"New land where?"

"Florida, I guess they call it."

"He wants to go there?"

"Yes. I don't know why he wants to leave Georgia. This is the most beautiful state in the whole world. He makes me so mad. We could be so happy."

"Would you go with him?"

"Yes, I'd go anywhere with him, if he'd just ask me to marry him."

"What do your parents think about him?"

"Our families have been friends for a long, long, long time— way before we were ever born."

"Elizabeth, you are now twenty-eight years old. It's ten years later. What is your name now, Elizabeth?"

"I'm Elizabeth Simms."

"Where do you live?"

"Red Mill, Florida."

"What is your husband's name?"

"Robert Simms."

"Do you like it in Red Mill?"

"Yes, it's my home."

"Do you have any children?"

"Yes."

"How many?"

"Five. The baby's just small. She a little doll. I called her Mary Jane."

"You are now ten, twenty, thirty years . . . you are becoming older now. The children are grown. The children have left the house. You are now a very old lady, Elizabeth. Do you see yourself in the house?"

"Yes."

"You are alone in the house now. What's happening in the house?"

"I'm sad."

"What are you doing?"

"Looking at the pictures on the mantel."

"How old are you now?"

"Eighty-nine years old."

"And you're all by yourself?"

"No, poor Daisy."

"Who is with you?"

"Daisy, the colored maid. Ninety . . . she's gone to bed."

"Then what happens?"

"I'm not well."

"Something happens."

"I'm so tired."

"One day you stand in front of the mirror and someone hurts you. Who is it? Do you remember? Now we can talk about it. It's all over. No one can hurt you again."

"My baby."

"Your baby? What is he doing? Which one of your babies?"

"James."

"What is he doing?"

"Rifle."

"What does he do?"

"Catch his button . . . "

"And what happens then?"

"Ohh!"

"You're all right. You can't be hurt anymore. Do you remember what happens then?"

"Everyone, everyone's gone."

"What do you do? Where do you stay?"

"Here. This is my home."

"Is there a difference now? Do you look different?"

"Yes."

"Now, after he shoots, what happens?"

"I don't care."

"You don't care for what?"

"Don't punish him. It was an accident."

"You mean, he didn't mean to?"

"No, his jacket . . . the button . . . "

"But why was he pointing it at you?"

"We'd been having trouble with prowlers. My niece and the maid had been seeing . . . seeing dark shadows of a man prowling around the house, and he tried to get in and they had a shotgun in the hall, by the hall window, leaning up against the wall by my room."

"What did he do?"

"James had come home unexpectedly, come upstairs, and I was brushing my hair. I always took great pride in my hair. It was still pretty."

"I'm sure it was."

"James picked up the rifle. He was wondering what it was doing there, and he tucked it under his arm. I saw him in the mirror, over my shoulder. As he greeted me, the trigger caught in the button of his jacket pocket."

"And it hurt you."

"Yes, it hurt me."

"And then what happened? What did you do then? Did you see yourself after that?"

"Yes."

"How did you look?"

"Crumpled on the floor."

"But you were not really on the floor, were you . . . you, yourself?"

"I stood looking at myself."

"Then where did you go?"

"Wandered."

"Did you meet anyone you knew?"

"No, I was all alone."

"In the house?"

"In the house."

"How long did you stay that way?"

"For a long time."

"What was the next thing that happened to you after that?"

"A young girl came to the house one day, with two young

children. She was so much like I was when I was that age. A sweet little girl."

"So what did you do?"

"She seemed to like my house, my home."

"Did you know her?"

"No."

"Did you communicate with her before she came to the house?"

"I showed her my house."

"How did you know where to find her?"

"*I don't know.* I showed her my house, and when she came . . . when she came it was like living again. She made me happy."

"Are you her? Is she you? Or are you two different people?"

"I don't know."

"When you were in the house, floating around for awhile, did you at any time disappear from it, or not remember anything?"

"Yes, there was a time when I seemed to rest. There was nothing."

"And then what?"

"Just darkness, and then I showed this young girl my home."

"In between, did anybody talk to you?"

"No."

"Nobody came to talk to you before that young girl came?"

"No. In the house, people came. They wanted to look about the house . . . curious."

"But not to talk to you?"

"This little girl was different."

"Do you remember being a child again? After the darkness, the period when everything was dark and you rested, after that, do you remember being a child?"

"Yes, yes."

"How was it? How did you become a child from the darkness? How did you go from the dark period of rest to become a child again?"

"Baby."

"You remember a baby?"

"A baby was playing on a porch with a clothesline and some clothespins."

"What was the first thing you remember when you woke up as a baby?"

"A woman came out and picked me up and carried me indoors."

"And the years went by, and then you grew up, and then one day you told this girl about your old home, is that it?"

"Yes."

"Why did you suddenly think of your home? What made it happen?"

"She was so much like I was. Not her temperament. She was so, so pure and good, I guess you could say."

"So you decided you would want to remember."

"I wanted her to live in my house. It was our house together."

"Did you know that the house has since been torn down to make way for another house? Time has gone on. Are you aware of that?"

"No, they can't take my home away."

"You still own it?"

"Yes."

"And this girl who is now you, are you her? Are you going to live in her mind with her, as her?"

"I must. She gives me purpose."

"Did you know someone who was a postmaster when you lived in Red Mill?"

"There was a young man who wanted to be postmaster for a long time."

"What was his name?"

"Jeremy McDonald."

"Do you remember any of the people in Red Mill who were in the army?"

"There were many, many of our boys."

"Any officers that you can recall by name?"

"My son was an officer."

"Which one?"

"One fought for the Union Forces against his father's wishes."

"What regiment was he in?"

"Cavalry, Persing . . . Persing of Cavalry."

"Anyone in the Southern armies?"

"My son."

"Which one?"

"Allen."

"What regiment? What rank?"

"He was lieutenant, Confederate Forces. He was Lee's dispatcher. He was a fine loyal officer, wounded three times."

"He was a lieutenant, Cavalry or Infantry?"

"Cavalry."

I decided to bring June out of her hypnotic state. After all, it was our first session together, and I did not wish to overtire her. There would be time for another session the following morning.

When June awoke, she remembered absolutely nothing. She felt as if she had just had a nice long nap. I immediately questioned her about any knowledge she might possess, either consciously or unconsciously, about the Simms family, but it appeared that she knew nothing more than what she had already told me. "The only thing I know is what the old postmaster told me," June explained. She could not *now* recall the postmaster's name. She did not know what name Mrs. Simms was known by prior to her marriage.

I don't think June lied to me. She answered my questions immediately and without reflecting, in a straightforward manner. There was no particular reward in her coming to Pittsburgh to see me, nor would there be any publicity for a long time to come. June had nothing to expect in a material way from our working together, and I do not believe that her makeup was such that she would have enjoyed telling tall tales. When she denied any knowledge of the Simms family beyond what the old postmaster had told her, I took her at face value. I honestly had no reason to feel otherwise.

I questioned her then somewhat more closely about her own background. Married at fifteen and now the mother of four children, she had lived in only three places: in western Pennsylvania; in East Hempstead, Long Island; and again in western Pennsylvania. At no time had she taken any interest in the South or in southern history. None of her grandparents or other members of her or her husband's family are from the South, nor have they anything to do with the State of Georgia. She has never been to Atlanta. Yet June has always shown a great interest in the history of the War Between the States. She doesn't know why the Civil War period attracts her so much, but it all started when she was about eighteen years old. She read some books dealing with the period, without ever studying it formally. Her education ended at the high-school level. But she took night classes in such diverse subjects as interior decorating, psychology, history, and writing.

It was getting late, and I suggested that June get some rest.

The following morning we met again. This time she went under even more easily than the night before, which is not surprising since the second or third session in hypnosis does go easier than the initial effort. I quickly took her back to her own birth, and then fifty years before it. Once again we established that her name was Elizabeth. Then I reminded her that we had talked before and that we would continue our conversation about Georgia now.

"Tell me, Elizabeth, what street do you live on in Atlanta?"

"We don't live on a street."

"Do you live in the country?"

"Yes."

"What's the name of your place?"

"On a large plantation."

"What is it called?"

"Hill Place."

"Who are your neighbors?"

"Our neighbors are quite far away—across the creek."

"What's the nearest place to you?"

"The Simms plantation."

"How far are you from Atlanta?"

"Oh, that all depends on, if it's a hot day it seems longer."

"How do you go to Atlanta? By what conveyance?"

"Papa always says, 'Jacob, bring around the buggy.'"

"What sort of church do you go to on Sunday?"

"The Baptist Church."

"Has it got a name?"

"Just the Baptist Church."

"It doesn't have a special name?"

"No."

"What's the minister's name?"

"Reverend Harold Clemens."

"Do you know the mayor?"

"Yes, I like to tease him."

"What's his name?"

"I call him Tubby."

"Why do you call him Tubby?"

"Because he's so round."

"Well, that's a good enough reason; but what do the people call him? What's his real name?"

"Judge Boland."

"What is his first name?"

"I don't think I know."

"Boland, huh? Has he been mayor very long?"

"Yes, for a long, long time."

"What party does he belong to?"

"Women of the South, sir, do not indulge in politics."

"You do know who's President of the United States."

"Of course."

"Who is? Who is president now? Every schoolchild must know that, and you're an educated young lady. Surely you know who is now president. You've read about him. What kind of a man is the president?"

"A great man."

"What does he look like?"

"He's tall and handsome. A distinguished young man."

"Where does he come from, North or South?"

"From the South, sir."

"Is he a military man or a civilian man?"

"He was a military man of great distinction."

"What's the color of his hair?"

"A light blond color."

"What's your papa's favorite newspaper?"

"Georgia . . ."

"The Georgia what?"

"*Tribune.*"

"Talk to me about some of your fine friends in Atlanta. The people that come to your father's house—who are they? I know that you're interested in Mr. Simms, but you must have other friends, and your father must have some friends. Has he any friends who are in the Senate or in the House?"

"There are men who are much confused about our government and the way our country is being handled. They join my father in the drawing room twice a week."

"What are they talking about?"

"I don't know."

"What do they think they ought to do about the government?"

"I don't know. Something drastic must be done."

"Do you know any of the names of these people that come to see your father?"

"Generally, before they arrive, the womenfolk are allowed to retire."

"Do you know who the senator is from your state, in Congress?"

"Yes."

"What is his name?"

"I'd rather not say."

"Why? Don't you like him?"

"Not particularly. Last year he asked my father for my hand in marriage. I will not marry a man I do not love!"

When you went to Atlanta, did you do any shopping, buying goods and things and finery?"

"We went to Atlanta, Mamma and I and my cousin."

"What is the cousin's name?"

"Alice Jenkins. She lives in Virginia."

"Where in Virginia?"

"Norfolk."

"Do they have a house there?"

"Yes."

"What did her father do?"

"He was a bookkeeper."

"For whom?"

"Munitions firm."

"What is their name?"

"Jenkins."

"Is he an owner of it?"

"No, in the family some way, I guess."

"So your cousin and your mother and you went shopping in Atlanta. Where did you go? Where did you do the shopping? What place, what store? Tell me about it."

"In a big department store. That last time we went, Mamma scolded me."

"Why did she scold you?"

"You know the cute little stools where you sit down to relax? I whirled around them, and Mamma said it wasn't dignified at all."

"What's the name of the store? Do you remember?"

"Harry Millin's . . . on Main Street."

"Did you see any other stores?"

"Confectionery store."

"Do you remember the name of the place?"

"Mr. Willike's. He was always nice to me. He used to save two little pieces just for me."

"Did you have anyone living in Atlanta, any friends or relatives?"

"Mamma had many friends."

"Do you remember any of them? Did you ever visit any of them?"

"Yes, sir."

"Like who?"

"Mrs. McDennis."

"What's her first name, or her husband's first name?"

"I'm not sure. I was always instructed to call people by their last name."

"Mrs. McDennis. What does her husband do?"

"Foreman."

"In what?"

"On a plantation."

"Any girl friends?"

"Some of them are like cats. You ought to hear the way they talk about the new colt that Papa just gave me."

"Where did he get it?"

"It was born to Mr. Silver Black."

"Who is Mr. Silver Black?"

"He's a horse."

"Did your father have an attorney, a lawyer, to take care of his business?"

"Yes, sir."

"Do you remember what his name was?"

"Gaylord Linholm."

"And your father was Franklin Tibbits. You're eighteen now, right?"

"Yes, sir."

"What year were you born?"

"Eighteen two."

"You were born in 1802?"

"Yes, sir."

"What is your birthday? When do you celebrate your birthday?"

"August second. My mother says that's why I have such a violent temper, because I was born in August, when it was so hot."

"How long has the plantation been in the family now?"

"My great grandfather built it."

"What was his name?"

"Harrison."

"Harrison Tibbits?"

"Yes."

"What was your great grandmother's name?"

"Marie."

"Marie, and then their son would be your grandfather?"

"Yes, sir."

"What was his name?"

"I think my grandfather's name was Franklin."

"Your father is Frank, and you mother is . . . "

"Catherine."

"With a *C* or a *K*?"

"With a *C*. Father likes to tease her. He calls her Katie. It makes Mamma mad, but she doesn't stay mad at Papa."

"You were baptized in the same church that you always go to now in Atlanta?"

"Oh, yes, sir. It has been a great tradition in our family."

"Now, today, think of today now. People are talking. Do you think there'll be a war? What do you hear?"

"There is great unrest. Everyone is a little afraid to say things openly. Men are angry. They demand that something be done soon."

"Done about what?"

"Our taxes. The government is trying to force, they say because of the slaves, they have raised . . . they have raised all the taxes, put a heavy levy on everything. The plantation businessmen are up in arms about it. They are trying to drain our blood from us."

"Have you ever been to a place called Red Mill?"

"No, sir."

"Never heard of it?"

"No, sir."

"Now, you know this boy, Simms, real well?"

"Yes, sir."

"Do you like him?"

"I love him, sir."

"And he loves you?"

"Yes, sir. He declared his love."

"How do your parents feel about him?"

"They are most pleased, sir."

"Do you think the two of you are going to get married?"

"Oh, yes."

"How soon?"

"I want to get married now."

"Mmm, but you're only eighteen."

"It makes no difference. Robert wants to wait until he has a home to take me to."

"When will that be, do you think?"

"I don't know. Soon, I hope."

"And have you met Mr. Simms?"

"Oh, yes, sir."

"What is Mr. Simms's first name?"

"John."

"John? You mean Robert's father is named John Simms?"

"Yes, sir."

"Mr. Simms has just one son—Robert?"

"Yes, sir."

"Are there any other children?"

"A daughter, Evelyn."

"How old is she?"

"Twelve."

"And Robert is twenty?"

"Twenty-two."

"Have you met any other people at the Simms's house from town?"

"At teas."

"Like what?"

"The women from the women's group at the church."

"Did you ever meet any officers?"

"One very handsome young man."

"What's his name?"

"Lieutenant Colonel Michael Wrinceson."

"That's an unusual name, isn't it?

"Yes, it is."

"What's he in charge of?"

'He works in an office."

"In Atlanta?"

"Georgia."

"Cavalry or infantry?"

"Cavalry, sir."

"You've met him?"

"He came to the house one time. Papa was most pleased to see him and they both hurried into the library."

"Have you ever met any doctors?"

"No, sir."

"Well, when somebody is sick, who do you call?"

"Daisy always takes care of us if we're sick."

"Have you ever seen any boats or ships?"

"We went for a ride on the Mississippi on a big paddle boat."

"What was it called?"

"The *Lilly Belle*."

"Where did you go on her?"

"Up the river."

"To what town?"

"We went to Louisiana."

"What did you do in New Orleans?"

"We went to a big ball there."

"Who gave the ball?"

"Mr. and Mrs. Thornton."

"Do you speak French?"

"A little."

"Did you meet anyone in New Orleans, other than the Thorntons?"

"Handsome officers."

"Like who?"

"Paul . . . I remember their faces and their first names."

130

"Did you meet the governor?"

"Yes."

"What was his name?"

"I don't know. I suppose I forgot it because I didn't like him. He was a fussy old man, not one bit of fun."

"But you know the governor of Georgia. Surely you know him, in Atlanta. Have you ever seen him?"

"Yes, sir."

"What's his name?"

"I'd rather not say."

"Why, do you have anything against him?"

"No, sir. He comes to those meetings. We are not allowed to discuss who comes."

"You can talk to me."

"Papa says not to trust anybody. There are spies everywhere."

"I'm on your side."

"They have imprisoned quite a few of our men."

"Who has?"

"The government."

"Why would they do that?"

"They were trying to overthrow the government. The meetings are secret."

"Who would want to overthrow the government? Who is the leader who would want to do that? Is there someone in Washington who says that?"

"Mr. Seward. He's in the Cabinet."

"Your father doesn't like Mr. Seward?"

"No, sir."

"Are there any other cousins on your father's side?"

"There is a disturbance in the family."

"What happened?"

"The brothers . . . the plantation was left to my father. They don't correspond any more."

"Where did they go off to?"

"I don't know. They're not spoken about in our family."

"I see. Do you remember any other relatives in Atlanta, or in Georgia?"

"Aunt Genevieve Jenkins."

"Where does she live?"

"In Georgia, in the main part of town."

"And what does her husband do?"

"She's a widow, sir."

"What did he do before he passed on?"

"He was a boat captain, sir. He was lost in a storm at sea before Alice was born."

"When was Alice born? Is she younger than you or older than you?"

"A year older."

"So she was born in 1801 if you were born in 1802, and he was lost before she was born?"

"Yes, sir."

"How is the Norfolk Jenkins related to Alice Jenkins?"

"Cousins, somehow."

It was time to bring June out of her hypnotic state. When she awoke, she felt fine and was ready to go home to her little town in western Pennsylvania. A few days later, I heard from her again. There was nothing special to report, really, except a certain unrest she kept feeling, and a continuing, strong emphasis on a personality change that had begun after her return from Florida, and that somehow was becoming more pronounced as time went on. Moreover, June found herself saying and doing things that were completely out of character with her usual identity. Even her parents noticed this on the occasions when they were together.

Principally, June—that is to say, the old June—was somewhat timid and not likely to say anything without first thinking it over very carefully. The new personality was the exact opposite—tactful but sometimes painfully truthful, and if one didn't like what she had to say, that was just too bad. Many a family fight erupted because of pronounced opinions on this or that, expressed by the "new" June personality.

Gradually, however, Sam has gotten used to the changes in his wife, for he truly loves her. There are things that he doesn't understand, nor does he wish to understand them any further. He accepts them and has learned to live with them.

Whereas the old June was simply dedicated to her domestic chores, the new personality suddenly developed an interest in the arts—music, amateur theatrics, all these things became a part of her new interests, and despite the fact that June lives in a small town, far away from the mainstream of cultural activities, she is trying to read whatever she can get her hands on to keep up with the sophisticated world outside. To her husband, this is all right, even though he himself does not have such ambitions.

As time went on, the personality of the alleged Mrs. Simms, and of the "old" June began to merge into one new personality in which, however, the elusive spirit of the plantation owner's widow was dominant, or became more and more dominant as time went on. To be sure, June neither encouraged nor sought this change but, to the contrary, found it upsetting. In order to allay her fears, I briefly explained that I suspected a factual reincarnation memory, and, without telling her of any verifications, presented the matter merely as a possible hypothesis. I also assured her that there was no danger involved, and that if she wished to suppress the personality of Mrs. Simms in her character, she could do so by merely asking me to suggest this in one of our next sessions with hypnosis.

This June did not choose to do. Somehow she felt that it was her destiny to live with her prenatal memory and to make the best of it. Then, too, it intrigued her: in a life as placid and ordinary as hers, any form of excitement was welcome. With all her tragedies, the life of Mrs. Simms seemed a better thing to contemplate than the secure existence of June, the housewife in western Pennsylvania. If she could have the best of both worlds, so much the better.

I asked June to do no more checking into the subject of hypnosis or reincarnation and to avoid any books on the subject. I promised her to look into all the material at the earliest possible time, and when it was all finished, to tell her who she was, who she had been, and what the future of both personalities might be. This seemed to satisfy June, and from that time on I told her nothing beyond casual conversation on the subject in general. As soon as possible, I would come and visit her in her little town in western Pennsylvania to continue my search for additional evidence dealing with the two lives June had apparently led in previous times.

I heard from her again in early June. What had puzzled me all along was the possibility of June's experiences being attributable only to ESP, perhaps through precognition, as in the case of her dream prior to seeing the ghost town of Red Mill. I wanted to make sure that extrasensory perception could not answer all the questions.

One night early in June she had retired and somehow could

not sleep. The clock struck two as she felt a strange loosening of the bonds between her body and spirit, and she had the feeling that she was floating apart from her body. Looking down upon the bed, she saw herself lying on it. The filmy part of herself then faded away, and all at once she found herself standing in her parents' trailer.

Her parents then and now have lived in a trailer in Brookville, Florida, a considerable distance from western Pennsylvania. June had never been to this particular trailer. She stood there for a moment in what appeared to be a living room, and as she passed her father's room, she could actually hear him snoring. She then stepped inside to her mother's bed, bent down, and kissed her on the forehead, at the same time touching her mother's soft, wrinkled hand. At this precise moment, her mother opened her eyes, looked up, and said, "Junie, what are you doing here?" With that, June just faded away again and found herself back in her own house.

The next morning she passed it all off as a dream, thinking that perhaps her unconscious was trying to tell her she should write to her mother. Three days later she received a letter from her mother. In the letter, her mother described a dream she had had in which she saw June standing by her bed the night before, and then she suddenly faded away. This had frightened her, because she knew about June's heart condition. "And it was so real," she added.

June's mother uses a particular bath powder with a certain aroma. That morning, June's daughter Cynthia came into her room and immediately remarked that her mother smelled particularly good this morning. Had her father bought her some new bath powder for Mother's Day? But June had not used any bath powder or perfume that night at all.

Her mother, on the other hand, had gotten up after June had faded away from her bedside and made herself a cup of coffee in the kitchen. When she looked at the clock it was exactly 2:20 A.M.

I was not too surprised to hear of June's astral projection experience. Oftentimes, psychic people tend to have stronger prenatal memories than ordinary people. This doesn't mean the ESP is necessary to have prenatal memories but that the two faculties frequently go hand in hand. I suspect it has to do with the greater degree of sensitivity encountered in psychic people.

It was time to visit June and her family in her little town in western Pennsylvania, and I began to make all the arrangements. It meant changing planes in Pittsburgh and then being picked up at the little airport by June and her husband, but they were most eager to do so and invited us to spend the night at their home, since it would be impossible to return before the following day.

On July 30, 1968, we arrived after a somewhat bumpy flight from Pittsburgh. The little airport was exactly as I had imagined it, just large enough to accommodate small planes, and the country around it was rolling hillsides, wide open and inviting in its own peaceful way.

Sam and June drove us to their town, which was about a half hour distant. Their white house sat back from the road somewhat, surrounded by tall shady maple trees. In back of the house there was a hillside lot rising up to the edge of the woods. The two-story house is twenty years old, and it has a pleasant downstairs parlor and kitchen and several bedrooms upstairs. We were given the best room in the house and found it comfortable and quiet.

Later, when we made the rounds of the little town, we realized that this was far removed from the mainstream of city activity such as we had come from; nevertheless, this was a busy little town, wrapped up in its own problems. Perhaps these problems were enlarged by the people who created or solved them, but to them, matters involving a charity affair or the latest scandal were about the only things that created excitement, and excitement is what the American countryside lacks most.

June had very carefully concealed her own case of excitement from her neighbors, for she did not want them nosing in when her guests from New York arrived. Thus, it was unnecessary for me to have warned her not to talk to local newspapermen, for she had guarded our secret well. About the only thing June had ever done with the Florida experience was a fictional account of the Simms murder case such as she knew it, based entirely on the skimpy story told her by the old postmaster in Florida. I read her notes for that story and found that they contained nothing we had not already discussed. There was nothing in the story about reincarnation, of course, or about Atlanta or Georgia, only an extended account of the Simms family and, particularly, of how Mrs. Simms died by hands unknown.

June has for years tried to write professionally, and she has even used the services of a New York literary agent, but she has sold very little, unfortunately. It is amazing that someone who writes as colorfully as she does and who has a flair for poetry, nevertheless is unable to spell even the simplest words. This, however, does not deter her from continuing with a would-be literary career, even though she realizes that the chances for publication of her stories are slim. Truly creative in her own way, she finds the greatest joy in writing them and does not worry too much about whether they will eventually be accepted.

I had asked June to contact her father in Florida, requesting him to authenticate the existence of Red Mill, if possible. I felt that this type of information would not harm whatever we might obtain through hypnosis, since we had already discussed it consciously.

June's father, a total skeptic concerning matters of this nature, had done a pretty thorough job, and the results were somewhat distressing to June. It appeared that the old Simms place was located in the village of Anthony, in Marion County, Florida, two miles north of Oak, on Old Route U.S. 301, about seven miles north of Ocala. This village was founded prior to the Civil War and named after Susan B. Anthony, the famous supporter of woman suffrage.

The village today is partially in ruins. There are still some people living there but it is only a matter of time until they, too, will go elsewhere. Thus, what appeared as a ghost town to June many years ago is again becoming a ghost town.

The area is in north-central Florida and is perhaps best known for the tourist attraction of Silver Springs. The Chamber of Commerce in Ocala has no records of a village called Red Mill. As far as they are concerned, there never was a ghost town by that name. June would have believed that her experience was nothing more than a vision or a dream had it not been for the fact that her father had taken her and her children there. She remembers distinctly seeing a faded sign reading "RED MILL" hanging on the still-standing little red railroad station, but there's little doubt in June's mind that Anthony and Red Mill are one and the same place.

Depressed by the discrepancies in what she remembers as facts and what her father was able to obtain, she decided to leave the corroboration of her experiences entirely to me. She really didn't care whether it was all her imagination or reality. All she wanted to know was what it meant to her and her future and her family, and as long at it would not hurt anyone, she was perfectly content to accept my verdict, whatever it might be.

Shortly after we had arrived and settled down comfortably at June and Sam's home, I asked Sam for his own impression concerning the changes that had come over June after her return from Florida. He acknowledged that there had been a major change in her personality. For one thing, her sudden interest in the local community theater was out of character. She wasn't the kind of person who wanted to be an actress, but all of a sudden she wanted to partake in the stage plays put on by the little theater.

"Before her visit to Florida, she wasn't interested in anything, as a matter of fact. After she got back, she was interested in politics, something she never cared for before, and in archeology and other things that hadn't interested her at all."

Sam works as a laboratory technician at the local glass factory. He himself has had some psychic experiences and is not hostile to the idea of ESP itself. His father had psychic experiences before him, so perhaps there is a tradition in the family about that sort of thing. He himself had been born in the little town, and his father had come there as a child. His outside interests include forestry and the preservation of animal life in the surrounding area, which includes a large state park. Sam is not particularly concerned with such things as reincarnation memories, and he really hasn't thought about the results of Mrs. Simms' influencing the character of his wife. He takes it all in stride.

It had gotten late, and we decided to go to bed. The following morning, right after breakfast, I decided to have my first hypnosis session with June. The children were sent to play outside, Sam was at work, and my wife, Catherine, was still upstairs asleep. Except for an occasional bird chirping outside it was very quiet. Quickly June was under hypnosis, slipping back to her previous existence as Elizabeth Simms. This time June seemed particularly agitated by something. I asked if there was anything wrong.

"I'm afraid."

"Why are you afraid?"

"There is so much fighting."

"Who is fighting?"

"Robert and Michael, my son and my husband. Always arguing."

"What are they arguing about?"

"The plantation. Robert wants Michael to settle down, take over his responsibilities, and he won't. He hates the plantation. He loves his horses. He raises thoroughbreds."

"Tell me about the plantation. What is it called?"

"We don't have a name for it."

"How far is it from Atlanta?"

"Quite a ways."

"How many miles? How long does it take to go there?"

"A day and a half."

"Do you remember your father's plantation in Atlanta? What was that called?"

"Hill Place."

"How far was it from Atlanta?"

"Oh, about two hours' drive by buggy."

"Do you think that there will be a war?"

"Yes, sir."

"Between whom?"

"The states."

"Why do you think there will be a war?"

"It has to come eventually."

"You're thirty-five years old. You are living on the plantation. You are Elizabeth Simms. You are married. Tell me, is there a war on now?"

"Yes, sir."

"What kind of a war is it?"

"Between the North and the South."

"And how old are you?"

"I'm thirty-six."

"The war has been on for how long?"

"A year."

"Who is the governor of this state?"

"A southern woman does not discuss politics, sir."

"Whom would you like to see governor?"

"Our main interest, sir, is who shall become our president."

"Well, who should be?"

"Thomas Jefferson . . . there's someone coming."

"Who is coming?"

"Cavalry men. . . they have to go into the glades. A prisoner escaped . . . a very important prisoner . . . a Yankee."

"Then what year are we in now?"

"Eighteen sixty-one."

"You are eighteen years old. You are Mary Elizabeth Tibbits. What does the town look like? How much of a town is it?"

"There's not much of it. It's just a small town."

"How many people?"

"About a thousand, I'd say."

"What do they call the place?"

"Atlanta, sir. It's not a very big place."

After I had brought June out of her hypnotic state I began to question her concerning any knowledge she might have of life in nineteenth-century Georgia. I threw the name Tibbits at her. It made no impression. She thought she had heard it somewhere before but really didn't know for sure. I tried Hill Place. No reaction. I said, "Jenkins, Linholm, Boland." All I received in reply was a firm no. June's face showed absolutely no sign of recognition. Now I tried Seward. This seemed to ring a bell. "The only Seward that I would know anything about would be in history, something to do with politics." she said. How far, did she think, did Atlanta go back? "I haven't the slightest idea when it was settled," she replied firmly.

"After you came back from that Florida trip, did you discover any change in you?" I asked.

"It was just as if I had been asleep for a long, long time and I woke up, and I have a lot of living to catch up with."

"Where she had been a conformist prior to her trip to Florida, she had turned into a free-thinker after her return. In the six years since then, she has never gone back, however. That one and only visit to the house lasted about an hour and a half. During her stay in the house, she had found time to scan some of the yellowed papers in an old trunk in the house. Unfortunately, she had not taken anything along with her except for a few of the ledgers, which she had showed me during our first visit in Pittsburgh.

"Was there any difference in the way you would cook or in the way you would do certain chores?" I asked.

"Yes, as far as sewing is concerned, and then there was this urge to sort of feather my nest better, and I took a course in interior decorating, and things like that, but I seemed to know automatically how to make drapes, slip covers, even my own clothing, which I didn't do before."

Even though June's great-grandfather had been a sharpshooter with the Union forces, she had always had a sense of sympathy for the South. This existed even before her visit to Florida. She somehow felt bad that the South had lost.

Another strange thing concerned June's liking of clocks. After her return from Florida she had become increasingly conscious of time and had installed clocks in every room of her house.

It was time for lunch now, so we ended the session. That afternoon after June had rested somewhat, I put her again under hypnosis.

"You are Mary Elizabeth Simms. You are fifty years old. You live on a plantation. You are Mrs. Simms. So you know the instrument through whom you are speaking? Why did you come and seek her out?"

"So everyone would know."

"What?"

"That my home was a family home and a happy one."

"Is there anything that you want done to make you happier?"

"No, not right now."

"Are you planning to stay with her?"

"Yes."

"What was the town in which you lived in 1820 when you were eighteen years old? What was the name of the place? Was it Atlanta?"

"People called it that, yes, sir."

"In 1820?"

"Yes, sir."

"That's very strange, because the records do not show this. Are you sure it was Atlanta?"

"The other plantation owners called it Atlanta because of a legend. They hoped that the day would come when it would become the Golden City that once sank to the bottom of the sea."

"At the time, when you were eighteen years old, there wasn't any city yet, was there?"

"No, sir."

"What was it then, farm land?"

"Yes, sir."

"How many people lived around there?"

"There are quite a few plantations."

"Were there any Indians around?"

"No, sir."

"Where had the Indians gone?"

"They had been driven back into the marsh."

"Were they civilized or were they wild?"

"There are no civilized Indians, sir."

"You remember the name of the county in which all this was situated? The part of the territory?"

"County Claire."

"What was the main village, or main town, in that county?"

"There was a place where we could go to do our shopping, about two miles away."

"What was it called?"

"Well, it was called Atlanta."

"Were there any other towns further away that you can remember?"

"You could travel for miles and see just plantation land."

"How did people get there?"

"They came by carriage from Georgia . . . by paddle-wheel boats."

"On what river?"

"Generally down the Mississippi and then over across land."

"Wasn't there any railroad?"

"Not yet."

"When the railroad came, where did it end?"

"It went from Atlanta down through North Carolina, down through Virginia, all the same line."

"Now, Atlanta, was that the end of the railroad, or did it go further?"

"A little further, down to the tip of Virginia."

"In Georgia, what was the name of that place where the railroad ended? What did they call it?"

"A small town, Billings."

"And how far was that from Atlanta?"

"Not too far."

"Do you remember, sometime during your long life in that part of the world, any names of governors or of the mayors? Any of them?"

"There was a Calhoun."

"What was his rank?"

"Senator, I think."

"How about any of the people around the city of Atlanta, mayors, governors?"

"Well, there was Tubby."

"What was Tubby's name, real name, I mean, in the books, in history?"

"I'm so tired."

"Was he the first mayor of Atlanta or were there any others before him?"

"I believe Tubby was the second or third."

"How old were you at the time?"

"Eighteen or nineteen."

"You are living in Atlanta. It is 1849. How old are you now?"

"I'm thirty-nine."

"Tell me, who was the mayor in 1849?"

"Why are these things so important?"

I noticed an unwillingness to answer my questions, so I decided it was time to bring June out of hypnosis. She awoke apparently fully refreshed and again with no conscious memory as to what had transpired during the half hour or so that she had been under hypnosis.

On January 31, 1969, June again "visited" with her earlier incarnation in Georgia. This time, she recalled the name of a politician visiting her father's home: Quincy Cabot. There seemed to have been some connection between this man and a foreign government, June felt.

I instructed her not only to watch out for dream impressions, but also for anything that might come to her at odd moments while awake. To facilitate this, June put aside a few minutes a day for regular meditation sessions when she could be alone and relaxed.

One might argue that June, who liked to write poetry, was making these scenes up from her own mind, guided perhaps by her unconscious. Be this as it may, they are certainly correct for the time and situations given, and while not evidential in themselves, are interesting in evaluating the entire case.

"When the shutters were closed during the day's heat," June wrote down her impressions, "the darkened rooms were damp and cool with the smell of tree moss. A dull, flat smell it was. The afternoon nap in the cool, darkened rooms was a delight. The heat outside was so dry that even your nostrils felt dry, and the air hung heavy over the fields, and the men would glance up at the heat of the sun, beneath their wide-brimmed hats, astride their mounts in the field, and take scarves that hung around their necks and wipe the sweat from their necks and faces, and curse the heat. The air in the large rooms seemed to hang motionless all about us, and the house was quiet. The quiet footsteps of Daisy and Jacob in the hallway outside the large white room was the only thing that could be heard as we dropped gently off to sleep. Our heads rested against large, soft pillows. Papa called it 'The ladies pantaloon time,' shushed by Mamma. By this time we gratefully stripped to our pantaloons and undervests. It gave me a sense of freedom, and I wished I didn't ever have to wear those long, old dresses again. Mamma fussed and fumed and said I was no better than the animals God had placed on earth, and that they had to wear clothes He had given them, and theirs was of fur. One time I announced that some day I was going to wear my pantaloons riding at midnight, and Papa dropped his dish of mashed potatoes and Mamma choked on her cup of tea. Daisy just growled at me and shook her head, but I don't care. I just want to be free and ride—the wild wind about me."

I instructed June to continue watching for any impressions or visions she might have naturally but not to try to force any of this material from her subconscious.

Beth, as June now seemed to call her more and more instead of Elizabeth, was particularly reluctant to yield any more names or actual information concerning the visitors at her father's place. There seemed to be a sense of endangering people by naming them. Now, one might argue that that is simply a subterfuge, and that June consciously or unconsciously was simply playing a game in order to avoid having to give concrete information. I don't think so, because the character of Beth Simms does indeed fit in with the fear of compromising political names by naming them to me, a stranger.

Far more interesting was the change that was now taking place in June's whole personality. Thirty-nine years old at this time, she felt far younger. There was a sense of jubilation within her in being alive that she had never had before. She felt almost reckless and searched for something crazy to do. This was totally in contradiction to her "old" character. She felt like writing poetry, and she wrote some pretty good poetry. It was May, and spring was all around the house. Western Pennsylvania can be very beautiful around that time of year, and June loved those days to the fullest.

Impressions came to her all the time now, at irregular intervals. Some of them merely duplicated visions that she had had in September, October, and November of 1968, but they all contained only material that I was already familiar with. Now and again there was something new. The name Joseph Mayo, for instance. She saw him as a short, fat man in a gray suit with a wine-red vest, little hair, and small-rimmed glasses, together with a tall, stately gentleman, who stood on the porch of their large white colonial house in the South, and they talked.

On another occasion she saw herself halfway up the Simms staircase, wearing a long wine-red dress with a small black swirl design all over it. It had long sleeves and white cuffs with small buttons almost to the elbow. She was happy, humming to herself. She saw herself holding up the skirt of her dress just to the proper height. It seemed that she was about thirty-eight years old, with long hair that was wrapped about the top of her head into a large, soft bun. Again, she sees the small, fat man called Joseph, only the name Tubby seems to be associated with him now. She hears someone refer to a waistcoat and doesn't understand what the word means.

Then there was the word Gwinnett County and lush green fields, tall trees, and a Creek Indian squatting down at a rippling creek that flowed on endlessly through the fields and woods, and the Indian drinking the cool, clear water. His horse bends its head to drink of the water, too.

Another scene shows her a group of young girls in long full dresses, sitting and drinking tea from little cups and laughing and talking. She hears them speaking with a southern accent, and she registers some of their names—Mae Thornton, Anna Blake, Evelyn Simms, Pauline Pendleton, Mary Bawds. Then there is a trip to a department store on Whitehall Street in Atlanta, Georgia, and she somehow knows she is forty-eight years old.

More names rise up from her suppressed subconsious. Friends of her father, smoking cigars and drinking brandy, are seen in a vision in a large library. There are arguments among them, and their voices are loud. She hears some of the names. There is Jefferson Davis, a tall man with shaggy hair, Paul Bragg, Tom Pendleton, Harmon Gilmer, James Herald, Alfred Helm, Talbert Westcut, John Holt, and Jessica Jennings. John Holt seems close to the Tibbits family. He is from Norfolk, Virginia, as is Jessica Jennings. He is a mayor, and the year is 1820. She sees the image of a tall Confederate soldier, Captain Robert M. Simms, born May 18, 1823. He serves on Longstreet's staff.

A scene in Norfolk, Virginia, in a brick-faced colonial house at the corner of Willow Street and Church: President Monroe is being discussed by two men passing by in front of the building. They wear high felt hats, and the year is 1819.

Then again, she had something more to add to the circle of friends Mrs. Simms had known in Gwinnett County. There was an Agatha Tiffin who lived on a farm with her parents, Ethel and Paul; her father made wagon wheels. The year was 1833.

As I started to sift all this material to begin my research to find as much corroboration of June's impressions as possible, I decided it would be best to have one more hypnotic session with her. Even though a great deal of this knowledge was now in my own subconscious mind and one could argue the possibility of June's getting it from me, I felt that an additional session might also yield new names that were not known to me at the time. Thus I invited June to join me once again in Pittsburgh, and on June 23, 1969, she did just that. I quickly regressed her to the year 1820 and asked her to describe the place she lived in.

"Was there a city anywhere?"

"No, sir."

"What was the nearest village?"

"There weren't any villages. There was a trading post."

"What did you call the trading post?"

"It was just a trading post. Papa used to go there. He'd tell me a lot of stories when I was a little girl, about his trips."

"Now, if you wanted to buy something in a store, where would you go?"

"To the post or to Virginia."

"Where?"

"Virginia, Norfolk."

"Wasn't that far away?"

"Yes, sir, but my aunt lived there."

"But near the Hill Place, wasn't there anything nearer?"

"There was land as far as you could see, and crops, and green grass."

"What did they call the state?"

"Georgia."

"What was the capital of Georgia?"

"Why do you want to know?"

"Where did the governor of Georgia live?"

"I don't want to talk about it."

"Were there any Indians around?"

"Yes, sir, Creek and Cherokee."

"Were you friendly with any of them?"

"Yes, sir."

"What happened to them?"

"They were forced to leave."

"Who forced them?"

"I don't want to talk about things that aren't happy."

"Where did they go?"

"They were sent away."

"What happened to their land?"

"It was taken over."

"Now, when you were living at Hill Place in those days, did you ever write letters to anyone?"

"My cousin."

"What was her name?"

"Alice Anne Jenkins."

"Have you ever been to Norfolk?"

"Yes, sir."

"Did you like it?"

"Yes, sir."

"What did you like most about it?"

"All the fancy balls."

"Who gave those balls?"

"Friends of Papa, and Aunt Jessica."

"Do you remember the music they played?"

"Waltzes."

"How many musicians did they usually have?"

146

"Six."

"What sort of instruments did they play?"

"There was a harpsichord and a harp and a violin . . . "

"Do you remember some of the songs they used to sing?"

"One."

"Can you tell me about it?"

"Yellow the Blues."

"How did it go?"

"Yellow the blues, my girl, my girl. Yellow the blues, I love thee true . . . "

"Was there a regiment stationed in Norfolk in those days? Don't tell me what they said to you. Just tell me a couple of the names, all right?"

"There was a Lieutenant Arnold Himbrook."

"Was he in the infantry?"

"Cavalry, sir."

"Oh, and do you remember what regiment he served in?"

"No, a girl never cares about the regiment, only the soldiers."

"Was it a state regiment or federal?"

"State, sir."

"You went there often?"

"Several times a year."

"What kind of a house was it?"

"It was like a whole block; like a house all on one block, but there were different houses all fastened together, and it was all brick, with a big white heavy door and a big brass knocker."

"Did you ever have any silver coins?"

"I have a penny."

"What did it look like, that penny?"

"Eighteen fifty, a new penny."

"What's on it?"

"It's large, and it's brass."

"What's on the front?"

"I don't know. There's an eagle on the back."

"Is there something on the front?"

"I can't turn it over."

"Is the eagle just sitting there, or does he have anything with him?"

"He has something in his talons."

147

"Tell me, Norfolk is on the water, isn't it?"

"Yes, sir."

"Did you see any ships?"

"Yes, sir."

"Do you remember any of them?"

"The *Billy White*."

"Was that a civilian ship or a navy ship?"

"A civilian ship, hauled cotton across the ocean."

"Weren't there any warships in Norfolk?"

"I don't remember them, only the loading of the big bales, four-masters."

"How old were you the first time you went to Atlanta?"

"I'm not sure."

"Were you still a little girl?"

"No."

"You weren't married yet, were you?"

"I think so. It's like looking for something."

"Well, you know Atlanta is a big city, isn't it?"

"Not when I was there."

"What did it look like?"

"There was a train."

"A train?"

"A train in 1848 or 1850."

"And did the train not go any further?"

"No, northeast of Atlanta, I believe."

"What did they call that place? I mean, where the train ended."

"A *junction* of some sort."

"Was it then called Atlanta?"

"When the train went through, yes."

"Before?"

"No, not for awhile."

"Did it have another name?"

"Yes, but I can't . . . "

"Who was Uncle Tubby?"

"Joseph Mayo."

"What did he do?"

"He was the mayor."

"The mayor of what?"

"Of Mayo County."

"What year was that?"

"I don't know."

"Was this before Atlanta?"

"Uncle Tubby was the first mayor of Atlanta."

"Did you call your uncle 'Tubby'?"

"Yes, sir."

"What profession did he have before he became mayor?"

"He was a planter of tobacco, and he talked politics with the gentlemen."

"Now, when you went to Florida, how old were you then?"

"I was nineteen."

"And what was Florida called in those days?"

"It was territory that was to become Florida."

"Did you go down there by horse or by coach?"

"We went down by boat, paddle river boat."

"On what river? Or on the sea? How did you go down there? Was it on the sea or the river?"

"I don't remember. I know we docked. It was a river where we docked at in Anthony."

"What was it?"

"Anthony."

"What was the name of the boat?"

"*Sue Clarity.*"

"When you were living in the Hill Place, did your father ever have any friends in?"

"Yes, sir."

"Did you meet any of them?"

"Henry Payne."

"What did he do?"

"A lot of the men were plantation owners all over the South."

"Anyone else?"

"Alfred Helm."

"Did any of them ever have any rank?"

"Jefferson Davis came to the house."

"Why did he come?"

"The gentlemen used to gather for meetings and take turns talking over politics."

"Did Mr. Davis ever talk money with anybody, and finances?"

"Yes."

"Did he have anyone in particular who could help him?"

"Papa's overseer used to help quite a bit."

Beth seemed to tire of the conversation now, and I noticed that it was time to bring June out of her hypnotic state, but since I did not know how soon we could meet again, I discussed Beth's presence in June's body with her. To my amazement, Beth realized very well that she was living vicariously through another person. Even though that other person, in Beth's thinking, was also herself, she wanted to take over. I explained that it was necessary for June to remain herself to the outside world, but that Beth could merge her own character, her own desires and unfulfilled hopes and wishes, with the personality of June. Perhaps a stronger, better personality would then emerge for June. But this wasn't what Beth had in mind at all. She wanted to continue her own life, untrammeled by anyone else's. I made it plain that this could not be, explained patiently that I did, indeed, have the power to send her away from June's unconscious mind forever. In the end we compromised, and Beth promised to help June strengthen her own character, without, however, destroying June's own personality.

After June returned to herself, we discussed briefly whether there was anything she remembered, but as in all the previous sessions, she remembered absolutely nothing of what she had mentioned under hypnosis. The only thing new she could contribute was a strange feeling of suddenly having forgotten her knowledge of English, which had occurred to her a few times in the recent past. For a brief moment she had had the feeling that she was speaking a foreign language, although she could not really express herself in it. English has sounded strange to her ears at that point. Worried about her hearing, she had consulted an ear specialist, only to find that she was in perfectly good health as far as her hearing was concerned.

After June had returned home to western Pennsylvania, a great sadness overtook her. This was not the first time that June had felt depressed. Over the years, she had sometimes contemplated suicide, for no particular reason, and on one occasion she had taken a few more sleeping pills than necessary, but whenever thoughts of death had come to her, something or someone within her had changed her mind and cheered her up. Now June knew that it was Beth who didn't wish to lose her instrument of expression.

By the fall of 1969, the deep depression left her, and a more mature presence of Beth filled June's being. It was as if the two personalities had finally come to terms.

In trying to prove or disprove the accuracy of June's statements, I assumed that any intimate knowledge of early-nineteenth-century Atlanta would be unusual for someone of June's background. If in the process of trying to prove the material to be accurate I should find erroneous statements as well, I felt that this would not necessarily militate against the authenticity of the case.

I have learned over the years that those on the other side of life frequently find it impossible to remember details of their previous lives, especially when these details are not of an emotional kind. If, however, the percentage of hits were to be considerable, the case itself would, to me, assume the ring of truth, even if there were also misses and omissions. I would, in fact, be very suspicious of any psychic communication that proved to be one hundred percent accurate. No human being, whether in the flesh or in the world of spirit, is that reliable and exact. Here, then, is the evidence, insofar as I was able to verify it.

Hill Place, the name of the plantation somewhere in Georgia, must have belonged to the Hill family at one time, hence the name. The name Hill was prominent in Georgia in the first half of the nineteenth century, and in fact is still prominent in that state. One may only think of Senator Benjamin Hill, but there are many other Hills listed in directories of this area. A William Hill was a member of the Inferior Court in 1923, according to *Atlanta and Environs,* by the celebrated Georgia historian Franklin M. Garrett, published in 1954.

I was unable to locate the exact spot where Hill Place existed, but if, as June claimed, it took a two-hour buggy ride from what is now Atlanta, then it could have been much farther inland than I had at first assumed. There is also mention of a paddle boat on the river, and if this is the Mississippi River, it would be even farther west. I am firmly convinced that many of the data given under hypnosis are correct, but that the sequence may have been different from that given. It may very well be that there existed confusion in the mind of Elizabeth Simms, speaking through June, if indeed she was, causing various names to be attached to different personalities from those to whom they should have been, or transposing the dates. Out of this chaotic condition I tried to get some order.

There is prominent mention of a Judge Boland. In the earlier sessions he was designated as a mayor of Atlanta. He is also identified as the man whom Elizabeth called "Tubby," but in the later sessions, Tubby is referred to as Joseph Mayo, who was also a mayor. Here, then, are the facts.

The second mayor of Atlanta proper was Dr. Benjamin F. Bomar, according to the Atlanta Public Library librarian Isabel Erlich. This was in the late 1840s and early 1850s. But there were three generations of well-known physicians bearing the name Boland in Atlanta during the nineteenth century, according to Franklin M. Garrett, research director of the Atlanta Historical Society. On the other hand, there was a Judge Bellinger, who died in 1853. He was a legislator, a justice of the Inferior Court, and active in politics between 1820 and 1853, according to *Atlanta and Environs*, Volume I, page 361. But it was customary in those days to call any dignified individual, especially if he was of personal prominence, with the honorific name of "Judge." As a matter of fact, to this very day there are a lot of honorary colonels in Kentucky and other southern states. Could it be that Mr. Boland was not really a judge but only given this name as a matter of courtesy, or did the confused mind of Elizabeth Simms confer the title, rightfully belonging to Judge Bellinger, to one of the Boland family?

There was certainly confusion about dates. When the alleged Mrs. Simms speaks of the year 1820 in Atlanta, she must be mistaken, for the city as such came into being only in 1837. The land on which Atlanta now stands was owned and occupied by the Creek Indians until 1821, and there was no white settlement until then. The town of Atlanta was first called Terminus, because the new railroad, connecting the western part of the South and the Atlantic coast, terminated at this spot, in what was then DeKalb County. Later it was briefly known as Marthasville and eventually became Atlanta, so named after the well-known legend of Atlantis. But it is, of course, possible that, speaking in retrospect, the entity might have confused the dates. I have always found it true that those who have gone onto the other side cannot cope with figures, dates, and other details of time because there is, apparently, no such thing as time over there.

The description of Indians being driven from their lands is entirely correct. These were mainly Creek and Cherokee Indians. There is a hypnosis reference to a Claire County. The pronunciation isn't too clear, and it may well be that she meant to say Clarke County. This is the more likely, as I have found several members of the Hill family residing in that area in 1827. In the list of land lottery grants made to veterans of the Revolutionary War, published in Atlanta in 1955, there are also a Clay County and a Clayton County in Georgia. Both of these are not too far from present-day Atlanta.

In discussing the coming of the railroad, the entity referred to the date of 1824 and also mentioned two towns—Dancy and Billings, North Carolina. Neither of these two places was I able to locate, but the records are not very reliable, since small places often changed names in the course of time. There is, however, mention of a Senator Calhoun. While Miss Erlich did not think that the famed Senator Calhoun was ever active in Atlanta, I found to the contrary that he was instrumental in bringing the railroad to Atlanta, or what was then called Terminus. Although the final stages of this railroad were only completed after the senator died in 1850, he was indeed connected with the fortunes and well-being of the area in and around Atlanta. Reference to this is made in *Atlanta and Environs* by the aforementioned Franklin M. Garrett.

Since Elizabeth was thirty-six years old in 1861, she could not have been born in 1802, as she had claimed in the very first session we had, but must have been born in 1825. When she spoke of her life as an eighteen-year-old in Atlanta, which would make this 1843, she mentioned that it wasn't much of a town, that it was small, and that there were about a thousand people there at that time. This is entirely correct.

In another session she also mentions the Cherokee Indians as being active in the area, which is something the average person wouldn't know. Elizabeth gave Tibbits as her maiden name. I have been unable, to date, to locate a Franklin Tibbits, but the United States Census of Georgia for 1820 does list a Thomas Tibbits on page 147.

She referred to a Baptist Church as being the one she went to to pray, and the same church she was baptized in. It is true that the First Baptist Church was the most prominent church in Atlanta during the early days of that settlement. In a portion of the tape fraught with difficulties, I find upon replaying that she also mentions a Father Tillis as her teacher. The United States Census of Georgia for 1820 does list a Joseph Tillus on page 148. She mentioned President Jackson as having been in their house. The fact is that Andrew Jackson did come to Atlanta in connection with the redistribution of land formerly of the Cherokee Nation. This was in 1835, according to Mr. Garrett.

When speaking of the stores and establishments of the city of Atlanta, the entity referred to Harry Millin's Store on Main Street. According to the bulletin of the Atlanta Historical Society, there were an Andrew, James, and Thomas Millican listed in 1833 in DeKalb County.

As for the Simms family, with whom she later became involved, they are listed in various records. This is not surprising, since we know as a matter of fact that Elizabeth Simms did live in the house in Florida until her death. What is important to prove, however, is whether June is the reincarnated Elizabeth Simms. That the original existed is a matter of record. There are Simmses listed for Clarke County, Georgia, between 1820 and 1827. There is a Robert Simms also in the list of land lottery grants made to veterans of the Revolutionary War on page 63, and the United States Census of Georgia for 1820 gives a Robert, Benjamin, and James Simms on page 134.

Although I was unable to connect a Reverend Harold Clements with the Baptist Church, as claimed by the subject under hypnosis, there is a Henry Clements listed in the 1820 Census on page 29. Whether this is the right Clements I do not know.

Mr. Seward was indeed a prominent Washington politician, but I must discount knowledge of this name, since it is a prominent name that might have been familiar to June from reading books or simply from her school days.

On June 13, 1969, June sent me a typed list of all the names that clung to her memory in connection with her previous incarnations. I had not discussed any details of my findings with her, of course, and the list actually comprises both her dream/visions and conscious flashes of reincarnation memories. All the names that have occurred during our hypnotic sessions are contained in this list, but there are also a few others.

The name Harmon Gilmer appears. Gilmer is the name of an early governor of Georgia—during the time when Elizabeth might have lived in Atlanta. Among friends of her father's when she lived in Georgia, June mentioned also a certain Talbert Westcut. The Atlanta Historical Society Bulletin for 1931 lists a Tillman Westbrook as living in DeKalb County in 1833. June referred to the Jenkins family as being related to her own. There were many prominent Jenkinses in the register of land lottery grants made to veterans of the Revolutionary War, and they are also listed for 1827, the period under discussion.

The entity referred to a Whitehall Street in Atlanta that she knew. It is a fact that Whitehall Street was and is one of the main streets of Atlanta.

Dr. Benjamin F. Bomar had a store dealing in general merchandise on Whitehall Street in 1849. He was mayor of Atlanta at the same period of his life and also one of the founding fathers of the Baptist Church. These three factors together seem to indicate that perhaps June might have been referring to Dr. Bomar, rather than to Boland, when speaking of her Uncle Tubby, since a mayor can easily be called Judge as a matter of courtesy also. Bomar fits far more neatly into the facts, as brought out under hypnosis, than any other names close to what June had said, but it is entirely possible that she was confusing several persons with each other.

By far one of the most interesting bits of information concerns her naming of Gwinnett County. Franklin Garrett was able to confirm that Gwinnett County was created in 1818 and existed indeed in Georgia at the time that Elizabeth Simms might have been a young girl. How could a Pennsylvania housewife have such intimate knowledge of a state she had never been to? What's more, in her June 13, 1969, roundup of impressions she says, "Father buys supplies from a trading post in Gwinnett County, Georgia territory, in 1818." Gwinnett was in existence in 1818 and is now part of metropolitan Atlanta, so it is entirely possible that she confuses in her mind that later name of Atlanta, given to what was then only known as Gwinnett county, Georgia.

In evaluating the material obtained through hypnosis from

June and correlating it with her wakeful visions, one must inevitably come to a conclusion that there are three possibilities for explaining her amazing memories of another lifetime: Either she has obtained consciously or unconsciously material from books she may have read and incorporated this material in her own unconscious mind; or it is a fantasy and the product of wishful thinking about a romantic South she never saw; or, finally, we are faced with paranormal material. After careful consideration, I must reject the first two hypotheses.

As for the paranormal aspects, there again we are faced with two possibilities. Conceivably, she might have had a precognitive dream of her visit to the Florida house. Then upon entering the dilapidated mansion, she might have served as the medium to a resident ghost who, in turn, was able to express herself through her, and, in fact, possess her for a considerable length of time both in the waking condition and through dreams.

One final note to round out the picture: A short time ago, June's niece acquired a place not far from the old Simms house in Anthony, Florida. With her parents, she visited the "ruins" of the Simms house only to find the place still standing, although in shambles.

Thus the report of the house being totally gone was, to paraphrase Mark Twain, grossly exaggerated.

Not that it seems to matter, for Beth now makes her home in a small town in western Pennsylvania anyway.

✳

CHAPTER THIRTEEN

The Strange Case
of the Two Catharines

CATHARINE WARREN-BROWNE WAS BORN in Lancashire, England, daughter of a naval commander and descendant of an old Northumbrian family on her mother's side. Many of her paternal ancestors were naval officers, including Admiral Blake, and her family is highly respected in England. Many of her ancestors have sat in Parliament, some are noblemen, and her father was killed at sea in 1939 as a result of the Second World War.

Catharine led an interesting and unusual life while in England. On many occasions she had psychic experiences, ranging from the knowledge of future events to the ability to see ghosts and experience the uncanny in houses in which her family lived or where she was visiting; but her psychic experiences do not properly belong here, astounding though they may be. She had visions of events in the past, experiences with displacements in time that too were truly amazing.

The family is Catholic, and she comes from an area of England that is even today predominantly Catholic. Many of her friends have been priests or abbots, and she considers herself a very good Catholic to this day, even though she wonders why the Church does not pay greater attention to the reality of psychic phenomena. She knows only too well that these things are happening and that they are by no means evil or to be feared.

She and her husband had been living in an old priory in 1959 when his father died and left them to cope with estate taxes. Under the present government, English inheritance taxes are staggering; thus, the money left them by Mr. Warren-Browne's father was taxed to the tune of 92 percent. Under these circumstances they found it impossible to carry on life in England. They had to sell the house and farm, and in 1959 they came to America to start life all over at the ages of thirty-eight and forty-two.

When I met the Warren-Brownes in Hollywood in 1968, I found them to be friendly, unassuming people. Mr. Warren-Browne was most interested in his new program of boat-building, a career he had recently started, while Mrs. Warren-Browne was particularly keen on doing a novel about a period that she found herself strangely involved in—sixteenth-century England.

As a result of our conversations, I later went to England to follow up on some of the things that had happened to Catharine in her earlier years.

She has always found great comfort in her Roman Catholic religion, and when she moved to an old priory of the Knights Templars near Ross-on-Wye, she reopened the chapel with permission of the Church and had priests from nearby Belmont Abbey say mass there now and again. As a consequence, she received an authentic reliquary from Monsignor Montini, who later became pope. Although she had occasionally discussed the question of reincarnation with her monastic friends, it wasn't of particular interest to her one way or the other.

Now in retrospect certain incidents make sense to her, although at the time they seemed to be completely out of context and truly strange.

When Catharine was only thirteen years old, the family had a governess by the name of Miss Gant. Catharine's mother liked her very much because Miss Gant was very learned. The children did not like her because they found her to be a fanatic and given to holding forth on various subjects in history at the breakfast table.

On one such occasion, the conversation turned to the life of Henry VIII. A book about this king had just been published, and Miss Gant remarked that he had just been a monster, worse than Caligula. At this, Catharine became suddenly very agitated and remarked that she was wrong. "Henry was a misunderstood man," she said quietly. Her mother insisted that she apologize to the governess, but ignoring her own mother, Catharine went on to speak of the life of Henry VIII as if she had known him intimately.

"The subject is closed," Miss Gant said rather snidely. "He was a very unpleasant man, and God punished him. He died of a very horrible disease." But Catharine's father backed her up at this point and let her have her say.

In quasi-medical terms young Catharine now described Henry VIII's fatal illness, denying that he had ever had syphilis and in the process shocking her mother, and remarking that the king had died of obesity and a varicose ulcer in his leg that would not heal due to a high blood-sugar content.

Such knowledge on the part of a thirteen-year-old girl was amazing, but even Catharine thought no more of it at the time. There may have been other incidents bearing on the matter at hand but Catharine does not recall them.

In 1957 she was very ill, recuperating at a private hospital in Bath, England. Due to a fall, she had had some surgery and was on the critical list when a close friend, the Abbot Alphege Gleason, came to visit her at the hospital. He stepped up to her bed and said, "Poor Catharine, what are they doing to you?" Very sleepily, the patient replied, "Here is good Master Coverdale come to comfort me."

Her visitor was taken aback. "Master Coverdale?" he said. "You are a learned young woman, but I should have thought I might have been taken for Cranmer, whom I'd always admired," he replied with a smile. By now Catharine was fully awake and asked, "Who on earth is Coverdale?" Many years later she discovered that Dr. Coverdale was a preacher friend and protégé of Katharine Parr, one of the queens of Henry VIII.

Mrs. Warren-Browne has had eight pregnancies but, due to a blood factor, has only three living children. On several occasions she would be in good spirits right up to the impending birth. At that point she would break into uncontrollable tears for no apparent reason. On one occasion, she was asked by her physician, Dr. Farr, in Sussex, England, why she felt so depressed at this particular point when all seemed to be going so well. For no apparent reason Mrs. Warren-Browne replied. "She was healthy, too, but she died of puerperal fever." The doctor asked whom she was talking about, and Mrs. Warren-Browne truthfully replied she did not know, nor did she have any idea why she had made the remark. The doctor then proceeded to tell her that this disease no longer presented any threat to mothers because it had been brought under control through modern methods, but that it was indeed a fatal disease centuries ago.

Years later, research established that Katharine Parr did indeed die of that disease.

After Mrs. Warren-Browne's son Giles was born, she became very ill and had what she called waking dreams, in the sense that they were far more realistic than ordinary dreams are. Suddenly, she saw herself as a woman almost dead in a great canopied bed. The woman had long, red-gold hair. Then Mrs. Warren-Browne would come out of this state and feel very depressed and sorry for the woman she had seen in her vision, but she always shrugged it off as a rather fanciful dream.

Ten years went by, and if there were incidents relating to the period of Henry VIII, they escaped Mrs. Warren-Browne's attention in the course of her daily activities.

She has a good education, and her knowledge of history now is equal to that of anyone with her background, but she has never had any particular interest in the period of Henry VIII other than what any Englishwoman might have. As for Katharine Parr, the name meant little to her except that she recalled it from her school days as the name of one of the wives of Henry VIII. Beyond that, there seemed to be no conscious connection.

In September of 1968 she and her husband happened to be in Iowa. He had some business there, and she was working on a book off and on as time permitted. She owned a pack of alphabet cards, and as she went about her work, she kept finding these cards arranged to spell the word Parr. She had not done this, nor was anyone around who could have so arranged the cards. She recognized the name Parr and thought that perhaps it had something to do with an ancestor of her family's on her mother's side. For, a long time back, there had been some connection with the Parr family of Northumberland.

Since she had no one to discuss this with, she decided to try the method of divining by pendulum. She put her wedding ring on a thread, and to her amazement it worked. There was indeed someone present who wished to communicate with her, and being fully aware of her psychic past, she did not reject this notion out of hand. Instead she decided it would be more practical to have an alphabet to work with, so she got out her Ouija board, and despite her feelings that such a board represented mainly a person's unconscious mind, she decided to give it a try.

"Who is there?" she asked.

Immediately the board gave her an answer. "Seymour," it spelled.

"Are you my Uncle Seymour?" she asked, for she could think of no relative other than her uncle who might want to communicate with her.

"No," the communicator said sternly, "Tom Seymour."

It still didn't ring any bells in her mind. "Which Tom Seymour?" she asked.

There was a pause. Then the entity operating through the board replied, "The Lord Admiral."

This gave Catharine pause for thought, and then she decided to investigate this communicator more closely.

"When were you born?"

"Fifteen o three."

'Why do you want to get in touch with me?"

"Long have I waited," the board spelled out.

"What have you waited for?" Catharine asked.

The whole thing became more and more ludicrous to her. Her suspicious mind was ready to blame her subconscious self for all this nonsense, or so she thought. She knew enough about extrasensory perception to realize that there were also pitfalls that a sensible individual had to avoid. She wasn't about to fall into such a trap.

"For you, Kate." Now, no one has ever called Catharine Warren-Browne Kate except her father, so she was rather dubious about the genuineness of the conversation.

Immediately, she thought of what she had read that could have some bearing on all this. Years before, she had read *The Wives of Henry VIII*, but that had been in her school days. More to amuse herself than because she accepted the communication as genuine, she continued working the Ouija board.

The unknown communicator insisted that he was Tom Seymour, and that she, Catharine Warren-Browne, was Katharine

Parr reincarnated. The notion struck Mrs. Warren-Browne as preposterous. She knew, of course, that Katharine Parr was the last wife of Henry VIII, the only one who managed him well and who survived him, but she had never heard of Tom Seymour. It is well to state here that all her research in this came after most of the information had come to her either through the Ouija board or in dream/visions.

Today, of course, she has a fairly good knowledge of the period, having even decided to write a romantic novel about it, but at the time of the initial communications in 1968, she knew no more about Henry VIII and his queens than any well-educated Englishwoman would know.

The communicator who had identified himself as Tom Seymour advised her among other things that she was buried at Sudely. Now, Mrs. Warren-Browne had always assumed that Queen Katharine Parr was buried in the royal burial vault at Windsor, but upon checking this out, she found to her amazement that Katharine Parr had indeed been laid to rest at Sudely, an old castle at the border of Worcestershire and Herefordshire.

Later she was able to find references to Tom Seymour in historical records. She learned that Tom Seymour and the widowed Queen Katharine had married after the death of King Henry VIII. Their marriage had lasted about eighteen months. Afterward, she had died in childbirth. Tom had survived her by about a year, when he was executed as a result of political intrigue.

At the time of the first communications through the Ouija board, Mrs. Warren-Browne did not know this, nor did she know the name of the child, the only child, "she" and Tom Seymour had had. Tom referred to the child as Mary. Mrs. Warren-Browne very much doubted this, assuming that the child would have been called Jane, since Jane Seymour was Tom's sister and a close friend of Katharine Parr; however, research proved the communicator right. The child's name was Mary.

All during October of 1968 she felt herself drawn to the Ouija board and compelled to write down as quickly as she could whatever was given her by that means. She didn't want to believe the authenticity of that material, and yet she felt that in view of her earlier psychic experiences, she should at least have someone look into this and authenticate the whole matter if possible or reject it, if that were to be the case.

Thus in December of 1968 she contacted me. When we met the following spring, we went over all the communications she had had until that time. "What indication do you have that you are Katharine Parr reincarnated?" I began.

"Well, this is what *he* thinks," Mrs. Warren-Browne replied politely, "unless, of course, it is something from the subconscious mind."

"What are Tom Seymour's reasons to assume you are his long-lost Katharine?"

"Well, he keeps saying that he's tried to reach me for years, that he's been waiting and waiting, and I replied, 'Katharine Parr is dead. Why are you not together now?'"

"And how does he explain that?" I asked.

"They are on different planes, on different levels," she explained.

"But you were reborn because you were in a more advanced state."

The communications between Mrs. Warren-Browne and Tom Seymour went on for about a month. There was still some doubt in Mrs. Warren-Browne's mind as to the authenticity of the whole thing. On one occasion, the communicator referred to the date on which their child had been born. Tom had insisted that it was August 17. Mrs. Warren-Browne went to the library and looked it up and found that the child had been born on August 28 and died eight days later. The next evening she reminded her communicator he had made a mistake in his calculation. "No," Tom Seymour replied through the board. "We had the Julian calendar, you have the Gregorian calendar." Quickly she checked this and found that he was right. The difference of eleven days was accounted for by the difference of the calendars.

"Before this communication came, did you ever have any slips in time when you felt you were someone else?" I asked Mrs. Warren-Browne.

"Not that I have felt I'm someone else but that I have known places that I have been to."

"For instance?"

"Pembroke Castle. When my uncle took me there, I said to him, 'Now we are going to such and such a room, which was where Henry the Seventh was born, who was Henry the Eighth's father.'"

"And how did your uncle react to this information?"

"Well, he was of course surprised, but you see, if I had indeed been Katharine Parr, I would have known this because Henry the Seventh was her father-in-law."

"Is there anything else that reminds you of the fifteenth or sixteenth century?" I asked.

"Yes, many times I will catch myself saying something that sounds unfamiliar in today's use and yet that fits perfectly with the earlier period in English history."

"Any strange dreams?"

"Yes, but of course I would consider them just wishful thinking. Sometimes I would see myself wearing long gorgeous dresses, and it seemed that I was someone else."

I suggested we try a regression experiment, but since Mrs. Warren-Browne's husband was present and both were somewhat pressed for time, I felt that this was not the best moment to try it. We said good-by for the moment, and I promised myself to take the first possible opportunity to regress Mrs. Warren-Browne back into the period in which she thought she might have lived. There wasn't sufficient time the following day to call her back and to try my hand at regressing her then. Also, they lived quite a distance away, and it would seem impossible to ask them to drive all the way to Hollywood again. But my time schedule was suddenly and unexpectedly rearranged. An appointment I had made for the following morning was canceled, and so I felt almost compelled to pick up the telephone and call Mrs. Warren-Browne. I explained that I had some free time after all and would it be possible for her to come back again so that we could attempt our first regression session. She readily agreed and within a matter of hours she arrived in Hollywood. I then proceeded in the usual way to put her into deep hypnosis. It did not take overly long, for Mrs. Warren-Browne, being mediumistic, was already attuned to this process.

I first took her back into her own childhood, making sure that the transition to another lifetime was gradual. She had come alone this time, perhaps because the presence of her husband might, in her own mind, impede her ability to relax completely, something very necessary for a successful regression.

When I had taken her back to her childhood, she spoke in great detail of her home in England and the staff they had. I then proceeded to send her back even farther, and we were on our way to finding Katharine Parr.

"You're going backward into the past before your birth; way back, until you can find you're someone else. What do you see?"

"I see a home with stone . . . it's Sudely."

"Whom does it belong to?"

"Belongs to Admiral Seymour . . . "

"Do you see yourself?"

"Yes, I see myself."

"Who are you?"

"*He* calls me Kate. I'm terribly cold. I called the doctor, told him how cold it is. Dr. Tahilcus, he was so good."

"Are you ill?"

"Yes."

"What do you have?"

"A fever."

"Is anyone else with you?"

"Dr. Herk. He is the king's physician."

"Who else?"

"My sister, Anne, and Herbert, and Lucy Tibbett, my stepdaughter. Lucy was a poor girl. She didn't like me when I married her father at first. Then she grew very fond of me. Lucy was most faithful. Lucy and Anne kept our marriage secret. I'm so cold, cold, cold."

"How old are you now?"

"Thirty-six."

"I want you to look back now, see what happens to you. You recover from this illness?"

"No, No."

"What happens to you?"

"I go away. I die. I die. I knew it would happen."

"Where do you die?"

"At Sudely."

"What happens to you immediately after you die?"

"Tom is upset, he goes, I'm buried."

"Where are you buried?"

"At Sudely."

"In what part?"

"In the chapel beneath the altar."

"What is on the stone?"

"HERE LIES ... HERE LIES KATHARINE—THE QUEEN DOWAGER—BARONESS SEYMOUR SUDELY— Kate Parr—Katharine ... Katharine the Queen. I never wanted that irony."

"Who is buried next to you?"

"No one, no one. He was gone. He was gone, and I loved him and I was angry with him. The Protector told me he was seducing young Bess. I believed it for a time."

"Who was young Bess?"

"The king's daughter."

"Who seduced her?"

"The Protector said that Tom did."

"What is his name?"

"Edward Seymour, Tom's brother. Edward Seymour hated Tom. He hated Tom's popularity. He hated the king's love for him. He was scheming. They even denied me my dowager rights. I had several manors and I had dowries from my two husbands before— Lord Latimer, John Neville—good men."

"I want you to look at the chapel now. What is next to your tombstone?"

"Next to my stone ... It's beneath the altar, a wall, and it fell. It fell on Cromwell's men. Cromwell's men desecrated my tomb."

"Is it still there?"

"It was rebuilt in later centuries."

"Can you see the windows of the chapel?"

"It was an oriel window, but it's changed. I left because Tom is not there. They took his body."

"Where did they put it?"

"They took his body back to Wiltshire. His family took it. Tom came from Wilkes Hall, in Wiltshire."

"Is he still there?"

"I don't know. I haven't found him since."

"Do you see him now?"

"I remember him. He had black hair, dark blue eyes; he was always tanned. He was at sea a lot. His brother was a cold fish."

"When you died, what did you do immediately afterwards?"

"I remember looking at him. He was sad, and I was sorry that I had not trusted him."

"Did you see your body?"

"Oh, yes, just *as a shell.*"

'Where were you?"

"In my bedroom in Sudely. My spirit got up. My body was taken."

"What did your spirit look like?"

"How does a spirit look?"

"Did you wear clothes?"

"I suppose so. I suppose so, but they couldn't see me."

"Where did you go then?"

"I went to Hampton."

"Why?"

"That's were we had been so happy. I went to Hampton because Tom had liked it. He couldn't bear Sudely."

"Where is Hampton?"

"Hampton Court, and his house in Chelsea."

"Did anyone see you?"

"I don't know."

"What did you do there?"

"I looked around from room to room, but he'd gone. He went north to my home."

"What did you do then?"

"I went to Kendal."

"Where's that?"

"In Westmorland."

"What did you do there?"

"I looked around where I was born. And Tom *went* there. He went up there."

"Did you find him *there?*"

"I saw him but *he* couldn't see *me.*"

"Did you make any attempt to let him know you were there?"

"Oh, yes."

167

"What did you do?"

"Yes, I put my arms around him, and he shivered. He was sad, and he went to my cousin's. He went to Strickland."

"Where are they located?"

"On the borders near Westmorland."

"And you followed him there?"

"I followed. Then he went away. He had to go into hiding."

"Why?"

"His brother accused him of treason."

"What had he done?"

"Nothing. He had the affection of his nephew, the little king. He had never done anything. His brother accused him of trying to wed with Bess, which wasn't true. Bess was only fifteen. He just used to romp with her. He had no children, just one baby that I left."

"And his brother, Seymour, whose side was he on?"

"He was the Lord Protector, but the little king didn't like him. They kept him short of money, and Tom used to take a little money and give it [to him]. That's why the Lord Protector took the great seal to stamp the documents. He took it away from the king."

"Who did the Lord Protector favor for the crown?"

"Jane Seymour and his son. Not James Seymour. James Seymour was his brother . . . the king's brother. Jane, Jane, she was Jane."

"And what happened?"

"Jane Grey, Lady Jane, she was only a child. She was married to Guildford. He wanted to control the children."

"But how was the Lord Protector related to Jane Grey?"

"I think he was her uncle."

"Then Jane Grey had the right of succession?"

"Rather distantly, but she thought she was a niece of the late King Henry."

"And he favored her cause?"

"Yes, because he knew that little Edward would not live. He had the lung tisk."

"And he then helped Lady Jane to become Queen?"

"Yes, but it only lasted a few days. The poor child. They beheaded just a child."

"What happened to the Protector?"

"He was beheaded too when Mary came. Mary had her good points. Mary had grown sour, but she was a good woman."

"Did she marry?"

"Yes, she was a sad woman. If she'd married younger and been in love younger, she would have been a happier woman, but the Protector tried to kill Mary, and somebody counseled her to hide. Sawston, she hid at Sawston."

"What happened at Sawston?"

"They burned it."

"Yes, and what did she say after it was burned?"

"She said she would reward them and build them better. She was fond of them."

"Do you remember the name of the people that owned Sawston?"

"Huddleston."

"Were they Protestant or Catholic?"

"They were Catholic. The Huddlestons always were . . . I knew a Huddleston in another life."

"You knew a Huddleston?"

"He was a Benedictine priest."

"What was his first name?"

"Gilbert, and in religion it was Roger."

"Tell me this—after you left, after you couldn't find Tom, where did you go?"

"I wandered."

"Did you know you were dead?"

"Yes."

"Did it bother you?"

"I was sad to leave, sometimes content. I was happy in a sense but sad to leave, because somehow we couldn't find each other."

"Were you aware of the passage of time?"

"Not particularly. It seems I was aware of people coming, people changing. People came where I was."

"Where were you most of the time?"

"I don't know how to describe it. It was light. I think it was happiness, but it was not complete happiness."

"Was it a place?"

"It was not just one place. It was . . . it was space, but I could go on the earth."

"How did you do that?"

"I could just will myself. Just will, that's all."

"Now, this place you were in up above the earth, could you look down from it?"

"Yes."

"What did you see?"

"Just a great amount of people, people, places."

"And the place you were in off the earth, did you see people?"

"Oh, yes."

"Did you recognize any of them?"

"My grandmother, my grandmothers."

"Did you speak to them?"

"Yes, you don't speak."

"How did you hear them?"

"We think."

"And the thoughts were immediately understood?"

"Yes, and we could will things for people. We could help sometimes, but not always. Sometimes you would want to prevent something terrible from happening."

"And?"

"So we would try, but not always, you couldn't always. People don't understand."

"Is there some sort of law you had to obey?"

"I don't know. I don't know."

"Was there anyone who took charge? Any authority up there?"

"Yes, in a sense. You felt bound by something, by someone."

"Was it a person?"

"It was a rule."

"Who made the rule?"

"It came from someone higher."

"Did you meet that person?"

"Not really. We saw a great light."

"Above you?"

"Beyond."

"What was the light like?"

"It was clear, bright, bright light."

"Did you speak to the light?"

"Yes."

"How did it answer you?"

"It said to be patient, go on, try to help. I wanted . . . I wanted. I wasn't really unhappy, but I wasn't fully content."

"Did anyone tell you how long you had to stay in this place?"

"No, they said that I could go on farther, or try to help."

"What did you choose?"

"I said I'd try to help, because time doesn't seem very long. Later, when I looked down, I knew the time *was* long."

"Who asked you whether you would want to go on farther? Who?"

"The voice from the light."

"You couldn't see a person?"

"No."

"How did the voice sound?"

"Wonderful."

"Male or female?"

"Male, male."

"Did you question who the voice was?"

"No."

"Did you know who it was?"

"I felt as though it was from God, although not Him in person. I asked, had it asked something."

"What did it tell you?"

"I asked if I had done anything wrong, not to be there where the light was. What was wrong? And he said no, that it was not wrong, that I could choose, that I could choose if I stopped grieving, that I could go ahead, or that I could go back and help."

"If you went ahead, where would you go?"

"To where the light was."

"Did He tell you where that was?"

"Not in words. I just knew that it was ultimate, ultimate peace. I came back and mothered all those children, Henry's children."

"You mothered them?"

"Henry's three children."

"Did any of them ever see you?"

"When?"

"When you were dead."

"Oh, no, but I think that's why I came back."

"When did you come back?"

"I think I had come back so much later. I took care of a lot of children. The war . . . we took care of a lot of children."

"Now, how many years after you had died did you come back?"

"In world years, a long time."

"But you say you took care of children. You mean on earth?"

"Yes, I took care of a lot of Polish children in this last war [World War II]."

"You didn't come back between the time you were up there and the time you're in now?"

"I don't remember. I searched for a long time. I searched for him."

"For Tom? Did you find him?"

"I saw him, but I could never get close."

"He was not up there?"

"Yes, but he wasn't with me, but he seemed to be looking."

"But after his death, did he not join you?"

"Not closely."

"Didn't you ask for him to join you?"

"Yes, I did, I did."

"Why didn't it work?"

"I don't know. He'd look at me; he'd look at me very sadly."

"What did he say?"

"He didn't . . . I don't know."

"Did you ask the light to let you find him?"

"No, I just waited."

"Now, when you came back in your present incarnation, do you remember how you were born? Just before you were born?"

"I remember my mother. She was a beautiful woman."

"When it was time to go down again, did someone tell you when the time had come?"

"I felt it was the time. I seemed to be shown."

"What steps did you take?"

"I didn't take any real steps."

"Was it immediately?"

"No . . . I saw them, but I knew my mother before."

"How did you enter the child's body?"

"I don't think I did by myself. *I was suddenly there.*"

"And what was the first thing you remember?"

"The first thing I remember, they put me to one side because they thought I wouldn't live. They thought I was premature."

"At that moment, did you still remember your previous life?"

"No, it was so dark. There was noise, like I was going through a tunnel, terrible."

"Did you see anything?"

"It was dark and noisy."

"Did you see anything?"

"No, not until after."

"And then what did you see?"

"Then I was in a room. They wrapped me up, but they said I wouldn't live, and I thought, Oh, I have to go back!"

"You remember that?"

"I remember that, and I thought, I must live. I must live. I had died before, and I was going to be happy. I was going to. I'd waited so long, eighteen, twenty years, and then it was so short."

"When you came back, you could actually understand what they were saying?"

"Yes."

"You understood every word?"

"I understood the words. I was premature, and it was rather difficult."

"And did this knowledge stay with you during the first few months, or did it disappear again?"

"It went after time. It went until the time when I was two. When I reached two until I was six, a great friend from the *other place* used to come and sit by me. Every night he'd come and sit by me."

"You mean, dead people?"

"Oh, it was wonderful. He came from where the light was."

"And why did he come?"

"He used to talk to me. He was someone very, very great."

"Did you remember his name?"

"We didn't call him by name because he was divine."

"Was he your master?"

"He was, yes, you would say 'master.' He sat by my bed, and then I lost him."

"What do you mean by 'master'?"

"He was what we understood as Christ."

"Is there such a person?"

"Oh, yes."

"Is he the same as the historical Jesus?"

"I think people embellish things, but he is *Christ*. He is the son of a great spirit."

"Is God a person or is God a principle?"

"Perhaps I'd call it a spirit. I never saw God, but I knew that one day I would. I would see behind the light."

"Now, after you came back, had you forgotten these things?"

"I forgot, but sometimes you dream and remember. He left when I got older. I realize I was the cause of his leaving. I was disobedient. It was a childish disobedience, but he told me that I would find him again, but I would have to go a long way."

"Did you ever find him again?"

"No, but I will."

"Did you ever find Tom again?"

"I know that I will, because Tom is trying to find me. Before, he didn't *try* to find me."

"What about Tom? Where is he now?"

"He's waiting to be with me. The time will come."

"Do you think he will pass over again?"

"I think so, this time."

"Why did he have to wait so long?"

"He had things to do."

"What sort of things?"

"He had to wait. He had to *obey* someone."

"What about you?"

"I was widowed at eighteen. I was wed at sixteen to Lord Borough."

"How old were you when you married Henry?"

"I was thirty-two when I married Lord Latimer. I was married in St. Paul, Yorkshire. Latimer was a good man but headstrong."

"Tell me about Henry. What was he like?"

"He was really not as fierce a man as they say."

"How many years were you married to him?"

"He sought my company several times when I was in mourning. He knew me from when Jane was his queen. Jane and I were friends. Jane asked me to take care of her little Edward. Jane died in childbirth fever."

"How did Henry ask you to marry him?"

"He just asked me. He said that he would wed with me. I knew inside that he was going to ask me, and I was hoping that he would ask me to be his mistress, not his wife. I didn't want either, really. I wanted Tom. We felt safer not being married to Henry. A mistress he could pension off. But he didn't have many mistresses, really. He was rather prim."

"How old was he then?"

"He was about fifty-two; he was very, very obese. He was very handsome, virile."

"Now, when you were married, did you celebrate your wedding?"

"Oh, yes."

"What were some of the songs that were sung at your wedding?"

"*Green Sleeves* is one, and a lute song."

"Do you remember the words?"

"I remember some of *Green Sleeves,* not much. Henry wrote music. He wrote one they do not credit him for."

"What was it?"

"*Western Wind.*"

"How does it go?"

"'Western wind, when wilt thou blow? With the small rains . . . I caressed my lover in my arms and lie in my bed again.' Henry wrote that, but they missed it. They missed it, I know. Henry played the lute. He was very musical. He was a very clever man. He had a very hot, angry temper, but he was quickly over it. But Gardiner and Wriothesly took advantage of this when they wanted to get rid of someone; they would pick a moment when it was easy to get him angry. That was how he got rid of poor Kate Howard. She was foolish. She was not fit to be queen but he loved her. It was just an old man's love for a girl, and she was vain and silly but she wasn't evil. But they took her away, and they wouldn't let her speak to him. She wanted to speak to him. She knew he would forgive her, put her aside. Henry told me that."

"What had she done?"

"She had committed adultery. She had loved someone else all

175

her life, but she was flattered to marry the king, and you couldn't very well refuse the king's hand. But she should have told him. He begged her to tell him."

"And she didn't do it?"

"No, she was afraid. She was a foolish child."

"And was Henry upset by her death?"

"Yes, he prayed for her. He was angry. He went away. Gardiner and Wriothesly had hastened the execution. Cranmer and Austin. He didn't like the Howards, you see. The Howards were very powerful. He didn't like them, and Henry felt betrayed by them. He had two Howard queens."

"Which was the other one?"

"Anne Boleyn."

"Tell me, why did you pick *this* incarnation, *this* body, *this* person to speak through? Was there any reason, anything you wanted her to do for you?"

"I was vain. I believe I was considered a good woman, and I loved my husband and I loved Tom. But I had vanity, and I came back into a world which had frightening things. She has tried so many things."

"You mean the woman who has it hard?"

"She's a woman who loves beauty around. She loves beautiful surroundings. It happened at a time when she was young. When she was stupid. She craved for it. This would upset her vanity."

"This is your punishment?"

"Perhaps it is a punishment, but also I wanted to help those children."

I noticed that Mrs. Warren-Browne showed signs of tiring, and as time had passed rather quickly, I decided to bring her back into the present and her incarnation as Mrs. Warren-Browne. This done, she awoke without any recollection of what had transpired in the preceding hour. She felt well and soon was on her way home to rejoin her husband.

All the historical data given by her in the hypnotic state were correct. Some of these are perhaps available in history books, and other data, while available to the specialist in that particular period, are not readily accessible to the average person. Katharine Parr had been twice widowed before she had married Henry VIII. The names of Lord Burgh and Lord Latimer are historical, and her death in childbirth is also factual. After the death of Henry VIII, there was political intrigue in which Tom Seymour fell victim to the machinations of his own brother, the Lord Protector. The fact of Katharine Parr's being buried at Sudely and the account given of the flight of Mary Tudor to escape her political enemies are entirely correct. Mary did hide at Sawston Hall, near Cambridge, which was burned down by her enemies and later rebuilt in great splendor by the queen. Huddleston is indeed the name of the family owning Sawston, and the Huddlestons to this day are a prominent Catholic family. The reference to the entity knowing another Huddleston in this incarnation makes sense if one realizes that Mrs. Warren-Browne was friendly with Father Roger Huddleston in her earlier years in England. Father Huddleston was a Benedictine priest.

But more than the factuality of historical data given, the descriptive passages of life between births and on the other side of life are fascinating and match similar accounts from other sources. It may be difficult for a nonreligious person to accept the visit of the Christ to the young Catharine Warren-Browne, and yet there are other accounts of such visitations. Surely the possibility that the Master looks after his own is not entirely illogical or impossible, for even a nonreligious person will generally grant the historical Jesus his great status as a teacher and healer.

On June 4, 1969, the day after our last meeting, Mrs. Warren-Browne had a meaningful dream, which she proceeded to report to me immediately. The following night she had another dream, also tying in with the regression experiment. Here are her reports.

DREAM #1

I sleep badly, and was awake until after 3:00 A.M., so this took place between 3:00 and 5:00 A.M. It was in color, and voices appeared to be normal or real. We were riding through woodland or heath country, am sure it was Richmond, the Surrey side of London. I was still Latimer's wife. Lucy Tyrwhitt, my stepdaughter by Lord Borough, rode with me. We were with the King's party; he was hawking. There were bearers and hawk boys, hounds, etc. Tom was there, home from France; he and Henry wore the Tudor colors of green and white. I felt very happy; in fact, happiness permeated the dream. It was a wonderful morning, early and misty, sun breaking through,

177

the smell of crushed grass beneath hooves and gorse. I rode a gray; Tom rode beside me whenever he could, although Henry would keep bellowing for him. They were on terms of great friendship.

Henry rode an enormous horse, dark bay. He was very heavy but rode magnificently. We cantered up a grassy slope to a clearing, and Henry released his hawk. He removed her hood, undid the leash from jesses, and threw her. She darted up in circles, and we all watched. In a very few minutes, she had sighted her quarry, then pounced in to kill. Henry was delighted. He laughed and joked. They had laid wagers. Then, in turn, the others, Tom included, released their hawks. Henry called the hawk boy to him. The boy knelt on the grass, and Henry roared, "Don't kneel, damn you. We are all men out here." He chose a small merlin and gave her to me, showing me how to carry her on my wrist. He asked after Latimer's health. Very assiduously, I told him that he seemed better, though very tired, and that he was at home translating a Greek work. Then His Grace asked me to ride beside him, and he chatted and thanked me for riding out to Hatfield House to see the children, Prince Edward and young Bess. He was in high good spirits. He waved his cap, plumes waving, and called out, "We shall meet again, my lady, at Greenwich." He led his party off at a mad gallop, leaving Tom to ride with me and Lucy and a page.

I felt very free from care. Tom took the small hawk from my wrist and gave it to the page, and he, Lucy, and I raced one another up the slope. I felt aware in the dream of a breeze, and joked with Lucy at not having to wear the awful boned corset the women wore then. Tom said that a horse felt good after days at sea. and he was going to Syon house. I felt guilty for being so happy when my husband was at home, ill.

DREAM #2

I was back in the past, at Hampton Court, in what had been Jane's apartments. Katharine Howard had been beheaded months before. In fact, I knew that the King had been alone since her death. I was aware of the year in my dream—1543— and I was a widow; Latimer had died. I felt alone. Tom was in France about the King's affairs, and I wished that he were here. The King had sent for me, and I was afraid that I knew why he had sent for me. There was a noise outside, and the doors were flung open. The King and two gentlemen in waiting came in. I curtsied to him, and His Grace took my arm and raised me, saying to his men, "Leave me, gentlemen, I pray you. I would speak privily with Lady Latimer."

They left, and Henry led me to a window seat. He kissed my hand and held me by the arm, then kissed my cheek and said, "How fair thou art, sweet lady, and kind as thou art comely. Today I was at Hatfield, and my motherless boy told me of your visits." He was in excellent spirits. His rages after Katharine Howard's death were all gone. I felt almost choking with fear, as I knew what was to come, and yet I pitied him. He was a crumbling lion and ruled a turbulent country as only a strong man could. He said, "You could give me much comfort and peace, Madam Kate, and, who knows, perhaps more heirs for England." In the dream I felt at a loss for words. He went on, saying, "My offer does not please you? I thought to do you honor and ask you to wed with me, for truly I have grown to love you very dearly." I told him bluntly, being a North Country woman, that I had not expected this, and, while honored, also felt a little afraid to accept, seeing the fate of two of his queens.

He was not angry, but told me to " . . . have no fear." I had "twice been wed and widowed" and was "known to be virtuous," and that "no scandal could ever attach" to me; that I had "both intellect and gaiety." He asked me to let him know very quickly as time passed and he was aging, but felt for me as any stripling. "Be kind to me. Be kind to England." Now, what woman could resist a proposal like that? Even in a dream or centuries ago? Incidentally, he removed my widow's veil and tossed it on the floor. That was Henry. We walked down the long gallery, and in my dream I knew it was where Katharine Howard had run screaming to try and reach the King. Henry seemed to sense this and told me, "Forget what has gone before." We went into another room he called his closet, and he seemed very gay, almost boyish, and told me that I could refurnish the queen's apartments as I wished; the Exchequer was low, but so be it. I told him (North Country thrift) that I had loved Jane's apartments and hangings, and that I had brocades and hangings in storerooms at Snape if he would like me to use them. He told me I was the first woman who had not sought to ruin him. And that was the end of the dream, all very domestic and practical. I remember, his eyes were small and sunk in heavy jowls, but he still had remnants of his former handsomeness, though he limped. I was aware in the dream of being sad that Tom had not returned in time and that the only way I could refuse the royal offer without offense was to enter a convent, and that did not appeal to me. I also knew it would endanger Tom to refuse Henry and hope to marry Tom later; heads fell for far less.

Mrs. Warren-Browne has, of course, read a few books on the period by now, especially Agnes Strickland's *The Queens of England,* and *Hackett's History of Henry VIII,* but she has not become a scholar on the subject. Perhaps she needn't, having primary access to information scholars have to dig for year after year.

Is Mrs. Catharine Warren-Browne the reincarnated Queen of England Katharine Parr, last and happiest of the wives of Henry VIII? She does not claim to be, but I think that the evidence points in that direction. The manner in which the first bits of personal data were received indicates that they came from a source that knew well what the lives of Tom Seymour and Katharine Parr were like. I am satisfied that coincidence, unconscious knowledge, and other ordinary factors do not play a dominant role in this case.

※

CHAPTER FOURTEEN

What Happens Between Incarnations?

WHILE IT IS FASCINATING to delve into the question of previous lives or to ferret out traces of memories with significance to the present one, such as the payment of karmic debts, it is perhaps equally fascinating to investigate the state in between lives, the transitional period when one life on the physical plane has been terminated and another one has not yet begun.

In the case of Pamela Wollenberg of Illinois, who lived in Scotland in the early sixteen-hundreds, the subject spoke of the experiences immediately following her death by jumping from the tower of Huntingtower Castle. "What was your next memory after you had fallen? What is the next thing that you remember?" "I was in wind." "Did you see yourself as you were?" "Yes." "Where did you go?" "Nowhere." Following that, however, she traveled to the castle and to various places in the vicinity. As she floated through time observing people dressed in what to her were strange clothes, she was interested only in getting back to Scotland and to the loved one she had left behind. Eventually, she discovered Pamela Wollenberg, who reminded her of a friend she knew in the sixteen-hundreds. Somehow she was reborn in Pamela's body. No one, at least not to her knowledge, arranged this for her, nor was she told that she must go back to the physical plane.

In the case of Ruth MacGuire, the system seemed to work differently, however. According to her testimony in deep trance, she stayed "on the other side" for awhile, learning about her short-comings in the life she had just left, and eventually progressed to a point where she could go back and try again. The old man who had been her teacher during that period told her that the time had come for her to go back, even though she really didn't care to. "Well, I really didn't have any choice, you know. These things are all decided," the subject explained under hypnosis. "Just what happened?" I asked. "Well, he said, 'It's time now for you.' He said, 'What you do here, you've learned; you practice, you meditate, you get the right idea, the right attitude, but you can't know if you are going to make it stick until you try it in the world, and you have to try it in the world before you know whether you've really got it in your bones.'" "And how did they make you go back?" "Oh, they said, 'You have to be a baby,' and I said, 'I don't want to be a baby. There's nothing dignified in being a baby.'"

The subject then described being put to sleep, and remembered only taking some sort of dive or rather a spin, and the next thing she remembered was crying in her present mother's arms.

N. W., a lady in Michigan, contacted me with an account of amazing clarity in which she remembered not only a previous life, but also her previous death. The lady is a university graduate and was born into a family with a very religious background. During her formative years up to age eighteen, she was brought up on a doctrine of a strict, vengeful God, and was frequently told by her minister that she was doomed to hell because of her worldly outlook. Later she married a young man who became a minister in the Nazarene Church. Despite this, she always felt a rebellious spirit within her against the upbringing she was given, and five years before contacting me had begun studying other religions in order to learn more about the world she lived in. It was at the time when she had just come across the works of Edgar Cayce that the remarkable incident occurred that prompted her to contact me.

"One day I lay down on my bed and almost immediately went to sleep," she explained, "when I found myself in a long line of slaves. In my hands was a round dish. We were walking towards the place where each slave was being served his daily ration. As I walked I kept my head lowered. I heard someone behind me whisper. 'Don't do it! He will punish you. Don't do it.' I seemed to know better than to raise my head or speak aloud to answer, but I whispered, 'I must. I just can't do what he demands of me.' The next thing I knew I was running down a tiled corridor, past two guards, in what I think was Muslim dress, through a curtain, where I saw two men sitting on cushions, deep in discussion. The guards were already advancing toward me. I tried to beg for attention and didn't succeed in being heard in the commotion. The master, the man I recognized as my master, had jumped to his feet and was berating me for interrupting him and his guest."

It should be noted that such clarity of detail is most unusual with ordinary dreams and nearly always points toward genuine reincarnation memories as the source. Mrs. W. continued her report to me, just as she remembered it the following morning.

"Next, I knew I was at the end of this corridor, and I had been severely beaten and was lying there suffering terribly. I heard a noise and saw my master and his friend coming out of the room. He ordered the guards to bring me to him. They came to me, grasped my arms above the elbow, and dragged me toward him. I heard myself say, 'Please, I beg of you; you're hurting me. They dragged me to him and dropped me to the floor at his feet. I saw he had a long slender knife in his hand. I had never seen one like it before and I wondered what it was. I heard him talking to the other man but I didn't hear what he said. He then pulled me to a kneeling position, talking as he did, bent my head over, put his left arm firmly around my head while he knelt at my left side on one knee. I could feel him shaving my head at the base of the skull. I wondered what he was doing. I tried to speak. He said, 'Be quiet.' He didn't seem to be angry. Suddenly he plunged the knife into me and severed my head from my body. I screamed as he plunged the knife in and suddenly stopped. I wondered why it didn't hurt anymore and why I had stopped screaming. Then I said to myself, 'Of course it doesn't hurt anymore. I am dead.' But I could still see what was going on. He had taken the inside out of my head, the part that my present knowledge tells me was my brain, and was showing it to his guest and explaining something to him about my brain."

At that moment Mrs. W. awoke, and as she did she heard herself say, "And that is why I always have migraine headaches when I'm under pressure or distressed. Now I needn't have them anymore." As a matter of fact, during the year following this remarkable dream, she has had only two headaches and both were caused by other illnesses. All through her teenage and adult years she had suffered from one to three migraine headaches a month, and was under medication for them, until that dream. There is another thing that seems to tie in with the flashback dream. Mrs. W. has a long birthmark at the base of her skull which turns an angry red whenever she has a headache. She is firmly convinced that the dream represents a true experience in a past life. Her husband, unfortunately, does not share her views. As a minister, he objects to the notion of reincarnation, even suggesting that his wife might be misled by an evil spirit!

It is interesting to note that the subject had no difficulty observing the moments immediately following death. Similar descriptions have been given by others, even those who died violently. In *The Search for Bridey Murphy*, by Morey Bernstein, both the principal subject and a deceased priest report their continued and largely unchanged existence immediately following physical death. In both cases they are able to observe what goes on around them, including the funeral arrangements. Similarly, the release of the etheric body from the physical counterpart seems in no way to impede the sensory ability of the personality, proving, of course, that the seat of consciousness is in the etheric body and not in the physical shell.

Alma Bartholic lives in a small town in Texas. She is in her late forties and was born in a small backwoods village in West Virginia. Asked to describe the environment in which she grew up, she described it as "rutted roads, narrow lanes that were tree lined like in an ancient country." When she was old enough to understand such things, her mother told her that she had been born with a veil over her face, meaning with psychic leanings. As a matter of fact, Alma has at times been able to foretell the death of individuals. But she's not truly psychic in the sense that she has significant and frequent experiences. However, as far back as she can remember, she has perceived a scene in her mind that made her wonder about reincarnation. In particular, Alma wondered whether we pick our parents or are ordered by someone over there.

"I remember being very tired, really out of breath, as if I had worked awfully hard on something. I was sitting on something soft, white and hazy like a cloud, and thinking, now that was not so very hard, but I'm glad it is over. Then a person stepped up to me and said, 'You are here,' I said, 'Yes, I just got here.' This other person said, 'Well there is someone else you have to be, you are going to another couple. I was reluctant but this person said, 'Look down, there they are walking out that lane together.' I looked, which seemed from a great distance down. I could see them plainly. I was higher than a building, like maybe just floating in the air. I can't define this. I wasn't in an airplane until 1961, so I'm sure it wasn't a daydream."

Mrs. Bartholic wonders whether her death in one life hadn't come awfully close to rebirth into another. There was something else that seemed indicative to her of a previous life. She cannot swim in her present existence and has a distinct feeling of having drowned at one time; also, at times when she is just about half asleep, she has visions of being burned alive and can even hear the dirt being thrown down on the coffin she is in. This has troubled her for many years and has given her parents some anxious moments.

If Mrs. Bartholic's life had been cut short by drowning and/or being buried while not quite dead, her return to the physical world might indeed have come comparatively quickly. Being shown one's prospective parents is rare; I recall only a handful of such situations. But it would appear in this case there was some sort of need to explain the rapid return of the soul, and perhaps reassure her that she was going to some very nice people.

Bernice M. lives in Georgia. "I really do not believe I have ESP or that I am neurotic," she explained to me as she described some early incidents of a psychic nature. Since most people with authentic reincarnation memories are not generally very psychic, an exception to that assumption would be of considerable interest. At age three, Bernice saw an apparition floating toward her bedroom from another room in the house her parents then occupied. The figure wore the clothes of an earlier period but was plainly visible to her. At age eight, her grandmother took her to visit some cousins in Pennsylvania. As she stepped into the parlor, she observed a man with white hair lying in a coffin. At the same time she noticed a sickly smell. Rushing from the room, she complained bitterly to her grandmother about being taken to a house where there was a dead man. Her grandmother assured her that there was no dead man in the house. Years later, however, her grandmother admitted that the house she had visited used to be a funeral parlor. Undoubtedly, Bernice had psychometrically picked up an image from the past. At age seventeen, an uncle with whom she had maintained close relations passed away. Immediately after his funeral he came to her in a vision, explaining that he wasn't really dead in the conventional sense. But despite these very marked incidents involving extrasensory perception, Bernice's reincarnation memory seems undoubtedly genuine. In some ways it links up with the case reported earlier.

"The first memory I have is of being in a misty place and not looking like myself at all," she explained, "I was there with three men. I cannot tell you their manner of dress. I was wearing a long blue-and-red dress and had my hair piled on top of my head, and was very tall. I spoke to the men and asked, 'How long will I have to stay here?' They said, 'Oh, you will see, you will go back in no time.' I don't know how much time passed, but they came and told me, 'You must go back now.' I said, 'But I've only just arrived.' They said, 'We know, but it is time for you to go back.' I don't remember my birth. I do remember being about three or four months old and lying in my carriage and looking up and seeing the sky and the trees and saying to myself, *it is true, I am alive again.*"

Just as in the previous case, Bernice M. also has a vague memory of being dead once and lying in her coffin and, in her case, screaming at people, "I'm not dead." But they did not hear her. Since childhood, she had always known that she lived before; it seemed part of her, like breathing. When *The Search for Bridey Murphy* appeared, Bernice was about twelve years old. She could not understand why so many people denied the truth in the book. To *her* it seemed natural that everyone had lived before.

It is rare, however, for a person to recollect large segments of an earlier existence in the physical world, and it is even rarer that they recollect their earlier lives from the beginning—that is to say, from birth onward. Occasionally there are examples of a recollection in which the person does actually recall his or her own birth.

In general, average people may remember as far back as their early school years. I, myself, have exceptionally good recall but I cannot remember anything before my third birthday. Although there is a dim memory of having been to kindergarten and having just turned three, this is not a continuous memory at all but merely a tiny flash in which I see myself in this existence. Now, this is not a reincarnation memory but represents a good memory, such as many people possess in the normal course of their lives.

Ordinarily, people do not recall details of their own lives before such an early age. I am not aware of any case in which a person recalls his own birth; except, of course, the one I am about to relate, but I am sure there must be others of a similar nature in the annals of psychic research.

Mrs. Nancy Anglin comes from Alabama. She is thirty-nine years old, married to a professional musician, and is a licensed practical nurse. They have one son and live in one of the cities in Alabama. Her interests are normal—music, the arts. They have an interest in reading books but there has never been any particularly strong interest in the occult or in psychic research. This is the more amazing as Mrs. Anglin has had, all her life, incidents of extrasensory perception, mediumship, and clairvoyance. She has taken these events in her stride without undue anxiety or extraordinary stress. Her ability to foresee the future and recall her impressions will be recorded elsewhere. Here I wish to concern myself solely with the amazing reincarnation memories she has had.

As a matter of fact, calling them reincarnation memories is technically incorrect, since in this case I believe we are not dealing with an earlier lifetime but with the beginning of this incarnation. Ever since she was a small child and able to speak, Mrs. Anglin has insisted to her mother that she can recall the moment of her birth into this world. She vividly described the day she was brought home from the hospital, a sixteen-day-old baby. I questioned Mrs. Anglin about the details of this extraordinary memory.

"My birth memories consist of an awareness of being blasted into a place where extremely bright lights and what seemed like the resounding echoes of human voices were imposed on my small person," she explained. "I vaguely seem to remember a detached observance of this affair, including blurred visions of figures clothed with masks and caps. The day I was brought home I remember riding snuggled in the arms of a woman with light brown hair and a prominent nose, arriving at a house where my Aunt Jeff and sixteen-month-old brother were coming out the front door, onto the front porch, I suppose to greet my mother and me. I did remember it was the first time I had seen trees, and was impressed by them. More clearly than anything is my memory of observing my mother, and in the thought language of the newborn, wondering, Who is she? What am I, and who are those people standing on the porch? Since I have been a young child I have always had the feeling of total detachment from myself and others, as if I were on the outside looking in."

Now, one might argue that Mrs. Anglin manufactured these impressions of her own birth at a later date, either consciously or, perhaps, unconsciously, from her normal knowledge of what births are like, but this is not so in this case, for we do know that her remarks concerning her birth go back to a very early time in her life when, being a small child, she had no access to this kind of information. Also, her impressions and descriptions of her own birth are so vivid and so detailed that they seem to indicate an authentic personal experience.

The more we understand the period "in between" lives, the more we will understand how reincarnation works. It is clear already that every case is different and must be judged on its own merits. Yet, there are undeniable parallels in the reports coming to us from widely scattered sources, sources that have no contact with each other, no way of comparing notes or of discussing their individual findings with each other or with a third party. In this respect, we should think somewhat more kindly of the fanciful notion found in many religions that there is a heaven populated by people sitting on clouds, who sometimes can look down on earth and see what goes on among mortals.

CHAPTER FIFTEEN

What Exactly Is Karma?

"KARMIC RELATIONSHIP" and "paying off old karma" are terms bandied about frequently among esoteric people (those who are interested in the occult, psychical research, and astrology). But the average person doesn't quite know what the term *karma* means. The word itself comes from India and signifies something like "accumulated destiny." Possibly there is a link between the Indian term *karma* and the Greek idea of *caritas*, derived from Karys, the goddess of charms and destiny. Words like *caring, care, charity, charm, charisma,* the technique called *Charismatics* (an idea created by me) may be interlinked, if not in meaning, then in derivation.

But Karys was also the goddess of the occult, of certain aspects of the underworld, and, as such, ruled man's fate. Any discussion of reincarnation is impossible without reference to the karmic law—that law which governs the nature of each incarnation. The karmic law is the set of rules under which the system called reincarnation operates. It is not a law in the sense of human laws, with judges and lawyers arguing the merits of each case. Under the karmic law there are no appeals and no interpretations that may differ from interpreter to interpreter. The karmic law is more comparable to a law of nature, such as the law of cause and effect, the law of attraction, and others found in the existing universe.

There are no exceptions from natural law; what seems at times a breach or circumvention of natural law is merely an aspect of it that we haven't fully understood. In time, we will understand such strange workings of natural law to the point where they no longer are strange to us. I am speaking here particularly of some psychic phenomena that are seemingly in contravention to conventional physical law but are in fact merely extensions of it in areas where we do not possess sufficient knowledge.

The karmic law has several important aspects. It operates impersonally, regardless of who may be involved. Since it plays no favorites and is not emotionally tinged in any way, it cannot be manipulated to favor one or the other. The karmic law is not written in textbooks or contained in physical reference files. It exists beyond time and space in an orderly fashion. It has existed from I don't know when, and it is referred to in many cultures at various times, independent from each other, yet no one has ever seen its scrolls. About the nearest thing to an orderly "filing system" are the so-called Akashic records. These records are said to contain the destiny and accumulated lives of everyone on earth—past, present, and future. The great seer Edgar Cayce referred to them in his trance readings; and lesser prophets have referred to the Akashic records whenever they have given so-called "life readings."

While I doubt the ability of some modern psychics to consult these records at will and extract information regarding former lives for individuals, I wonder whether the great Edgar Cayce may not indeed have been right in stating that these records do exist. There seems to be a need for some sort of central clearinghouse if man's destiny is truly an orderly process. The Karmic Law would be very difficult to administer if some record were not kept of the individual's deeds in each incarnation. Thus while I cannot say that I know where these records exist, I feel that they may well be a reality in the nonphysical world. Interestingly enough, Tibetan tradition speaks of a similar record in existence in a remote monastery in Tibet, where every person's life is recorded and where previous incarnations are also listed. If such a book exists on the physical plane, no trace of it has yet been found, but then there are many things that exist of which we know nothing *as yet*.

How do you acquire karma? If, as we assume, karma is the accumulated or acquired fate credit—either positive or negative, as the case may be—then there has to be a point at which an individual has no karma at all. Unfortunately, we arrive at the same unanswerable point where all religious philosophy must arrive sooner or later: the condition *before* the law took effect.

Every action man takes, everything he thinks, says, does—whether on his own initiative or in response to another person's—is capable of being evaluated on merit. Some deeds or thoughts can be classified as good, others as bad, and others as indifferent. Common logic tells us this. However, from the karmic point of view, it is not enough to judge man's activities along conventional lines. Every action and reaction must also fit into the greater scheme of things. The karmic law asks whether the action undertaken by one individual helps or hurts another individual; and, conversely, whether the activities of another individual create positive or negative factors in the receiver. First of all, karmic law concerns itself with impact on other individuals. Secondarily, it deals with the impact of action or thought on other elements in nature, beginning with animals and extending right through to everything in creation, whether animate or inanimate, if indeed there be such a distinction. (Recent research efforts seem to point to a needed reevaluation of our concepts of what constitutes animate in nature and what inanimate is.) In other words, a person's thoughts and actions are viewed not from *his* point of view, or even from the point of view of the one who may be the receiver of that activity, but from a much higher reference point, as if the observer were way above the action, looking down upon it, removed from it personally but involved in it as a scorekeeper. Although there is some evidence that specially "trained" discarnates are assigned the task of evaluating human action and enforcing the karmic law, justice does not rely entirely on the actions of human beings, even of those who have gone into the next dimension. It appears that the law operates autonomously in that every single action or thought by an individual registers in the "central registration office," the storehouse of universal knowledge, the Akashic records (if you wish), the focal point of administration where everything is known simultaneously and eternally, both forward and backward in so-called time.

Karma is acquired continuously by everyone. No action is too insignificant, no thought too fleeting, nothing too small to weigh in evidence when the balance must be restored. That moment, of course, is rebirth, a moment when retribution or reward is in order. No one can avoid creating or acquiring karma. Karma itself is like magic: it is neither good nor bad but depends entirely on the one creating it whether it is good or bad in the long run. This tantalizing thought presents itself as a partial explanation for the complexities of human personality: There are many opportunities laid out for a person at the moment of birth, encased in a denser outer layer called the physical body, and every action and reaction, every thought and feeling are counted toward the next incarnation. They are, in fact, the equivalent of human personality. Or, to put it more precisely, a person's personality is not a monolith but a loosely constructed combination of stimuli, thought, feelings, actions, reactions, attitudes, and interludes held together by the ego-consciousness: the pilot of the human personality vehicle. On this basis everything happening to one small particle of the whole may have important repercussions for the rest of the structure. This is shown in nature by the fact that individuals can be greatly influenced by comparatively small and short-lived incidents in their lives. Even major deeds need not take more than a few seconds, yet may have lasting effects for the rest of that individual's life, in that particular incarnation. The amount of so-called time spent on certain actions or thoughts is quite immaterial in relationship to the impact.

Some comparatively slow developments, consuming much time, may still have only very limited meaning in terms of karmic value. It takes only a few seconds to murder another human being, but the impact will stay with the perpetrator for the rest of his years. On the other hand, one may strive for many years to gain a certain advantage or goal, yet this effort will only weigh very slightly in the evaluation at the end of that individual's life. It is not even the honesty or sincerity with which one applies oneself to any given task. After all, human talents and abilities differ greatly. Then, too, we must consider that a life without previously acquired karma is merely a theoretic assumption.

For practical purposes, and in order to understand the workings of reincarnation, we should begin with the earliest life on earth during which some previously acquired karma already exists. The question is, where does such karma come from? We have no evidential information concerning the number of incarnations possible for each human being. As I have already pointed out, the evidence for transmigration or the change from animal to human status is practically nonexistent in scientific terms. Yet, something must have preexisted man's first incarnation as man. I have no concrete solution to offer except the feeling that perhaps prior to a fully structured and individual personality, man may have drawn upon the forces of the environment to create karmic preconditions. From the *second* incarnation onward, the matter is much easier to grasp. Quite obviously, the actions and thoughts of the first lifetime in a physical body as a human being will determine what happens in the next incarnation. From then on it is a matter of action and reaction, determined by a rigid sense of values that differs greatly from the conventional human set of values.

Nobody can avoid acquiring karma, since without karma there is no life on earth. What man can avoid, however, is to acquire *bad* karma. Those who hold no beliefs in reincarnation will not see the need to do so, of course. It is their privilege to discover these truths at the proper time when, unfortunately, they will be unable to correct things except by obeying and subjecting themselves to the very law they thought did not exist. But those who have learned that a system called reincarnation and karma exists and affects them can to some degree determine the shape of things to come in their next cycle on earth.

This does not mean that one need live a moral, strictly controlled life, dedicated to humanitarianism and the denying of the self. It is nearly impossible for most human beings not to acquire some negative karma as well, even if there is a conscious effort to avoid it. We are, after all, emotional creatures, and at times allow our lower instincts to run unbridled. On balance, however, the knowing individual can leave one lifetime with a vast surplus of positive karma and need not fear that the next incarnation will present him with too great a bill for the wrongs he has done in this one. Avoiding bad karma requires, however, that the individual be conscious of his responsibility not only to himself as an instrument of divine expression, but also toward all of his fellow men, his fellow creatures, and the entire environment. The degree of responsibility toward the world in which one lives determines very largely the conditions in the next return. Unfortunately, a large part of humanity is unable to grasp these very simple truths. The universe cannot function as a wholesome and harmonious creation if some elements in it persist in abusing it. It must therefore eliminate such elements by the natural means inherent in the karmic law.

Certain thoughts and actions are obviously negative in character, even if the individual involved is not cognizant of reincarnation evidence. To kill, to cheat, or to abuse another human being or an animal, to steal or destroy property—all of these actions are not only morally wrong in terms of our conventional society, they are equally wrong in terms of the universal law and karma.

But the obvious breaches of law are not the chief cause of so much karmic debt: it is in areas that are not easily recognized as being negative that most of the negative karma is acquired. Studied goodness, organized charity, actions designed to ease one's conscience rather than stemming from spontaneous feelings do not help one's positive karma at all. On the other hand, actions or refraining from actions that would interfere with the harmony in nature or in a fellow human being can weigh very heavily in one's favor.

Those religions that speak of a Judgment Day are merely personalizing a continual appraisal going on under the karmic law. How do you avoid negative karma? Consider yourself a vehicle of divine expression, in that you have been put on earth to perform a certain task or tasks. Do not assume that there is not a definite mission or purpose involved, for nothing in nature is accidental or wasted. By assuming that you have a job to do, determine what that job may be, and once you have found it, do it as well as you are able. In knowing what you are all about and implementing that knowledge to the best of your ability at all times, you are coming closest to fulfilling the spiritual purpose of your existence. Your own inner barometer will tell you when you are on the right track or when you are off it. There is a certain feeling of satisfaction in knowing one has done something well or that one has done the right thing. Those who do not have this ability as yet within themselves can develop it by learning to be calm and, at times, introspective. Sooner or later, the ability to sense what is right or wrong does come to everyone. Action taken intuitively is more likely to be correct from that point of view than logically dissected and weighed action influenced by the logical mind, environment, upbringing, and other external factors. *Feelings, of which intuition is a part, are a direct pipeline to the reservoir of truth.*

In this connection it is not wrong to seek personal advantage or success on any level, but it is wrong to seek it to the detriment of others. To look for fulfillment on *all* levels is not only right but the natural and instinctive expression of a fully developed human being. To seek such progress through the destruction of others however, is wrong.

When the opportunity presents itself to advance without destroying someone in one's path, then *that* is the positive karmic thing to do. Critics might argue that it is almost impossible to succeed in the world without stepping on or over someone else. The answer depends on the circumstances and the ways: for instance, if a clever businessman, through his own resources, acquires the capital to buy out a competitor, that competitor will have to look elsewhere for his professional fulfillment. Had he fully utilized his own resources, he would not have been bought out. The same businessman using immoral or illegal tactics to undermine his competitor while the competitor is doing everything within his abilities to advance himself would yield the same end result of course. The competitor would be bought out by the stronger man, but the means used to attain this end would have created negative karma.

I am not suggesting that everyone must look out for his fellow man in order to progress. Everyone must look out for himself, to begin with. Only when a man *consciously* or, by default, unconsciously causes harm or destruction to another being does negative karma come into effect. On the level of human life itself, through violence and fear, one might argue this point of view to the extreme: How does a soldier performing his patriotic duty to defend his country and kill an enemy compare to the murderer who kills a man for his money? Does the motivation determine the evaluation of the outcome? In my opinion, the taking of life, especially human life, is *always* negative karma. War and violence themselves are carriers of negative karma; consequently, all actions taken as part of such activities can only lead to the acquisition of bad karma— whether the individual concerned does so for seemingly lofty motives or not. In the words of George Bernard Shaw, "There are no just wars."

Those who advocate a completely prearranged universe devoid of all free will may argue that the selection of activities leading to bad karma may also be predetermined for a certain individual. A Genghis Khan may have been chosen by fate to be an instrument for its own ends. Is it his fault that through his cruelties he acquires enormous amounts of negative karma? I am not a believer in total predetermination but feel that a degree of free will is open to all of us. It is this very important amount of decision making that creates karma for the next incarnation. Thus, if a Genghis Khan committed himself to the role of conqueror, with all the inherent destruction and cruelties, he did so because of a sense of destiny born from his own desires or frustrations, and not based on the inner call that alone determines a man's proper expression in each lifetime.

How do you pay off karma? As we have seen, karma can be either a credit or a debit, depending upon the nature of the event, situation, action, or character of the individual involved. If it is a credit, then it will be paid off automatically through the intervention of the karmic law in due course. If it is a debit, it will have to be wiped out in the next life through positive actions and reactions. Contrary to the popular slogan "opposites attract," *like* attracts *like* in the esoteric world. Good karma brings forth more good, and it seems axiomatic that the payoff for positive karma is an increase over the previously acquired good karma. The extent of this differs from case to case. The status quo is not in keeping with the universal aspect of life: everything moves at all times. Positive karma will not be paid off by negative karma in a subsequent incarnation. But positive results in one lifetime must be based upon corresponding positive factors in the previous one or previous ones. *In other words, everything must be earned.* An individual may or may not accept the karmic payoff in good grace, but he cannot prevent the discharge of karma from one incarnation to the next. The idea that someone may refuse to accept the good is not as far-fetched as it may sound: Some individuals, out of extreme modesty or more likely out of a psychological fear that they cannot properly reciprocate, are in the habit of rejecting good things coming to them. With karma, there is no choice. There cannot be any choice, since the law operates naturally, impersonally, directly, without the intermediary of a human element. Even if an individual wanted to reject the blessings stemming from previous positive karma, to whom would he address his complaint? Not to the deity, since the deity creates the law but does not administer it. Not the "Board of Directors," as I like to call them—those advanced souls who have been entrusted with the supervision of an orderly progression from one lifetime to another. They have charge of operating the karmic law but they do not have the right to suspend it.

Advanced individuals who understand this law can build from one incarnation to the next until they reach the highest levels; at which point they may elect to become members of the elite of beings, sometimes called the Masters. To be sure, one does not accumulate good karma deliberately, in a cold-blooded, cunning, or planned fashion. Rather, one accumulates it by being in tune with the spirit of the universe, by *training oneself to react* instantly and intuitively in the right way, no matter what the challenge or situation may be.

Thus, the matter of acquiring further positive karma is not one of logic but one of feeling. Feeling, in turn, cannot be acquired at will the way one acquires a bank account. It is a delicate expression of soul that results when the trinity of mind, body, and spirit are in harmony, exercising a maximum of interaction and utilizing in full the force inherent in it from the moment of its creation. In popular terms, knowing oneself: understanding one's potentials, strengths, and weaknesses, and accepting oneself with all the faults that may be present; while at the same time placing oneself at the disposal of the forces of fate, realizing that one is but a small particle of a large and unified system, and being alive in the fullest sense of the word—those are the sure methods by which one increases positive karma.

If one has done something in one lifetime that must be classed as negative karma, it will have to be paid off in some fashion in the next life. Occasionally, it may take several lifetimes to be fully paid off, or the neglect, the negative factor stemming from one incarnation may only be paid off several incarnations later. Every case is individual and different, but one thing is sure: Bad karma must be paid off *eventually*. This is how it works: If an action has been committed in one lifetime that comes under the classification of negative karma, the same situation will not recur in the following lifetime or in one of the next incarnations. Rather, parallel situations will be "thrown into the path" of the individual, to be acted upon by that individual as his free will dictates. Since the situations are only similar in terms of merit but not in terms of circumstances, the individual being tested cannot anticipate them or connect them with happenings in an earlier lifetime. He is, therefore, solely dependent upon his own resources, his good or bad judgment, as the case may be.

The only exceptions to this rule are the comparatively few cases where reincarnation memories, or rather small traces of them, have been permitted to remain. I have found that this is the case only when a lifetime has been cut short, or when some major situation in one lifetime has not come to fruition. Thus, such reincarnation memories seem to be in the nature of bonus arrangements, giving the individual a small head start in the next incarnation by allowing him some insight as to his previous doings. In this way, he may benefit from the information and apply the knowledge to parallel occurrences—if he is alert to the deeper meaning of the event, of course. Only those conversant with reincarnation theory can properly evaluate such links.

For instance, let us assume that an individual has made gains in his business by dealing dishonestly with a friend. In his next lifetime a situation may come his way in which he has the opportunity of dealing again with a friend in some totally different business matter. Sooner or later he will be put to a test: whether or not to take advantage of his friend. If he follows his natural instincts without also listening to the inner voice of harmony, he may simply do the obvious thing and take advantage of his friend. But if he is attuned to the deeper meanings of such challenges, he may reject the opportunity and come to his friend's aid. Instead of taking advantage of a faltering business by buying it out, he might lend his friend support so that he could go on with new strength. That would be discharging negative karma. The balance would have been restored.

Everything in the universe must be in balance, and that which is not must swing back and forth until its movement brings it to a point where total harmony reigns again. For when the forces of plus and minus are equal, they join each other and create a new whole, which is neither positive nor negative but contains elements of both. Polarity is that which separates, but it also creates the driving force to purify and eventually come together again. When full harmony is reached, polarity serves to keep the balance.

A particularly sensitive point in reincarnation research concerns illness in individuals when there is no apparent reason for such illness to exist. *Can illness be karmically caused?* Most illnesses are caused by a state of imbalance in the etheric body of the individual. Only accidents or diseases clearly due to neglect should be attributed to physical causes. But some, if not all, of these illnesses and accidents may be due to a karmic debt. In cases where an individual has physically hurt another, causing that person to be ill or crippled, the individual himself becomes similarly afflicted in the next incarnation. His suffering wipes out the suffering of the one he has mistreated. This need not be the identical illness or affliction but may be in a different part of the body; nevertheless, in its impact it would parallel the situation suffered by the other person in the previous incarnation. Do we then inherit the illnesses and afflictions of our previous sojourns on earth? On the surface, it would seem unfair for us to be responsible in this lifetime for something committed by our previous self, living a totally different life and being an entirely different person. Such responsibility and inherited doom smacks of the idea of original sin propounded by the Roman Catholic Church and rejected by the majority of progressive thinkers. But it is nothing of the sort. In being given a chance to make up for a wrong done by us in a previous life, even if it means suffering in this one, we are in the end ennobling our own soul, helping it to progress by eliminating the negative aspects from the past. If an illness or affliction has been recognized as karmic, it does not follow that we cannot do something about it. We can deal with it as if it were an illness caused by wrong thinking or an imbalance in our own system. The techniques in dealing with it are exactly the same, and as a result we may eliminate or overcome the karmically caused illness. By doing so we are not setting karma aside. The incidence of the illness or affliction itself is the karmic debt being offered for *payment:* our *efforts* expanded on in our own behalf to eliminate the illness or affliction is a proper positive response under the karmic law. By doing the "right" thing about our illness, we would be acquiring positive karma were it not for the fact that we are extinguishing an old negative karma. Thus the slate is clean; there is neither loss nor gain.

Karmic law operates through parallel situations, carefully

evaluating conditions in such a way that we are not given any hints that there may be a connection between what is happening to us now and what has happened to us before. Since the majority of people do not have reincarnation memories in the waking condition and only a fraction remember sufficiently in the dream state to be able to draw conclusions from their reincarnation flashes, we can only guess that some event in a past life may be responsible for our present predicament.

But one life must be lived at a time: Decisions and reactions must be based upon our personal feelings, regardless of how many lives we may have lived before. The karmic law would be meaningless if we knew that we were being tested or that some events in our lives were due to a similar event in another lifetime. Likewise, the karmic law would be without sense if we did not have free will in deciding, if only intuitively, what to do about every situation we are faced with. Man's free will is the very foundation of his kinship with the Deity: If he was created in His image, as the religionists claim, then it would seem a cruel persiflage if man could not determine his reactions when faced with the forces of destiny.

But bad karma to be worked off or good karma to be increased are by no means the only reference points from incarnation to incarnation. When there are traces of previous memories, they are in many cases due to *unfinished business.* Unfinished business may concern itself with a mission in one life that was cut short by tragic circumstances and could not be accomplished. It may have to do with setting things right in some way or it may refer to the carrying out of a trust.

Since unfinished business can range almost the entire width of human experiences, it is difficult to pinpoint the tell-tale marks of such causative factors. But there is present an overriding compulsion, a driving force to do certain things, to be in certain places, to seek out certain individuals or situations that cannot be explained on the basis of the current incarnation. As a matter of fact, in many instances it goes counter to present inclination. People of one type of background will seek out people of an entirely different background and feel completely comfortable with them, while feeling out of place with their own. This applies to places and occupations as well. Even skills acquired in one incarnation may be remembered, gradually or suddenly, in the next one if they were in some way not fully utilized in the earlier lifetime. This accounts for a number of amazing situations where individuals seemingly possess talents, interests, and inclinations for which there is no rational basis in their present circumstances.

But unfinished business may also pertain to personal matters; it may create difficult problems in one's emotional life. It may even create social and legal difficulties. How does one dispose of unfinished business? First, it is important to recognize it and to put it into the right perspective in relation to the present circumstances. Can one deal with unfinished business under the current circumstances, taking into account one's abilities, powers, environment, and obligations? If there does not seem to be any insurmountable barrier against it, the wisest thing would be to attempt to pick up where a previous lifetime has left off. The more one realizes the nature of the unfinished business, partially through snatches of reincarnation memories, partially perhaps by observing one's peculiar inclinations and unconscious activities, the more one can gradually put oneself into the shoes of the person whose business was left unfinished earlier. Using intuition as much as possible, circumstances will present themselves that demand certain reactions. If the synthesis between present personality and the remnants of the previous one is a good one, instinctive moves will be made and the unfinished business brought to a conclusion. It may not always be the identical business, to be sure; parallels are also common under such circumstances.

Either way, the matter is taken out of the karmic relationship and one is able to move forward in the present incarnation. Ignoring unfinished business when one has become aware of it is not advisable. To begin with, it won't go away. One cannot simply suppress it or look the other way, because the more one tries to avoid it, the more it is likely to establish itself in both conscious and unconscious minds. The advice of professional psychics in such matters is also of doubtful value; unless the psychic involved is of superior quality, such readings tend to reflect too much guesswork, generalities, pastoral advice, and otherwise useless material. Far better sources of information lie buried within oneself if one learns to tap such sources through meditation, periods of withdrawal from the world, and a progressive, steady technique of listening to the inner voice, which we all have.

Unfinished business is not due to an accident or neglect of nature. Nature does not err. But there are individual cases where proper application of the universal law demands an interruption of the business at hand, even though on the surface this seems unreasonable. If, as I assume, all data pertaining to an individual are read into a kind of spiritual computer, and this spiritual computer comes up with certain negative suggestions based on the sum total of what was fed into it, the smooth continuance of that individual's mission on the earth plane in this particular incarnation must be disturbed in order to satisfy *previously* acquired karma. Even the way in which we are born and in which we die is a karmic matter, determined by and dependent upon previous conditions and reactions. Theoretically, at least, only the "young soul," the soul just created by the "system" is relatively free from such burdens, since it comes into the cycle of life without previous testing. But even the new soul brings into its first encounter with life certain environmental factors acquired at the very moment of birth.

The question still remains: Who decreed the law of karma and who administers it? If we are to believe that God is contained in all of us and that we are a part of God, then it would appear that the karmic law was also in some way and in some measure created by us, the living universe, in order to have a set of rules to keep this universe in harmony and balance. It appears to administer itself by the very virtue of its infallibility; its omniscience makes it possible for the law to be aware of all that occurs everywhere forever and thus, quasi-automatically, to take the necessary steps to create the conditions that are likely to balance the system for specific individuals.

It may be a little like a Calder mobile, in which the delicate construction can be put into motion by a very slight touch. Eventually it returns to its properly balanced condition. The waves, that is to say the movements the mobile makes while adjusting itself and returning to its state of perfect balance, may be compared to the encounters between human beings and situations with which they must cope one way or another.

CHAPTER SIXTEEN

Destiny Encounters
and Soul Mates

VERY COMMON OCCURRENCES involving karma, both negative and positive, are the links between millions of people who do not know each other in the present incarnation. Many people have had the experience of meeting someone and having the strong feeling that they have known that person before, yet are unable to determine when and where their relationship began. Sometimes this recognition is sudden and dramatic. Some of these experiences are classed under the déjà vu phenomenon, because they give the feeling of "haven't I met you someplace before?" People meet for the first time and are able to describe each other's whims and likes instantly and without previous knowledge. Some people can remember having been together in strange places and under strange circumstances, yet, in the cold light of their present lives, there is no rational basis for their assumptions. This phenomenon is so widespread, so common, that it appears to me to be one of the prime elements in the reincarnation system. *Links* between people are important, but perhaps even more important is the *recognition* of such links. Undoubtedly, the majority of these links are simply overlooked, shrugged off as coincidences, strange occurrences without particular meaning, or are deliberately ignored.

I maintain that two people never meet without some significant purpose being involved. This purpose may come to fruition *after* the initial meeting or perhaps at a much later time; but two entities in this universe do not meet each other unless a third purpose is involved and meant to be dealt with. The difficulty lies in recognizing first that there is a link between them, and, second, what the purpose of their meeting is in terms of universal or karmic law. Those who have undergone some esoteric training will perhaps be able to recognize some of the meaning inherent in such meetings. But people who still cling to the materialistic concept of coincidence and accident in nature are not likely to see the deeper meanings behind such so-called "chance meetings."

Links of this kind are of the utmost importance not only in accomplishing one's mission in life, but also in furthering the other person's purpose. The more we understand the meaning and the meaningfulness of links between people, the more we begin to understand the meaning of the reincarnation system.

Sometimes the pursuit of links can be exaggerated. People who are firm believers in reincarnation may see deep significance in everyone they meet, everyone in their family and among their friends, to the point where the entire notion becomes grossly exaggerated. Mistakenly, they will attempt to identify everyone they know as having been a close friend or relative in a previous lifetime or perhaps several lifetimes ago. Thus, the present mother becomes a daughter in another life, the rejected lover was the successful rival in the last incarnation, the child who reminds one so much of one's grandmother is the grandmother reincarnated, and so forth. Return of a loved one or a friend between one incarnation and the next one is possible, of course, but recognition of such relationships must be based on *evidential factors:* certainly the life readings being dispensed by self-appointed experts for a specific sum of money do not offer such meticulous proof. There is no need to disregard scientific standards in this field, where such standards are the only safeguard against delusion, whether perpetrated by others or by one self.

If you meet someone and become convinced that you've lived before in the same place and at the same time, you must search for details of that life together that are capable of being checked out objectively in the files and records of various libraries and research societies. If the life together was in some distant civilization of which there are no research records, such as Atlantis or Lemuria, the matter of proof becomes very difficult, of course. But whenever you are dealing with a known civilization and time in human history, proof of the existence of certain individuals can be found in the majority of cases. Even if the individuals concerned were of minor status and thus not likely to be found in historical records, indirect evidence can be obtained through the knowledge of circumstances, ways of life, terms used for certain articles or conditions, and, in general, by carefully observing knowledge not otherwise explicable in terms of the individual's present circumstances and background.

As yet there is no question that relationships based upon previous lifetimes cannot seriously be considered as bases for close relationships in this life. While the interest in parapsychology and the occult sciences has risen in recent years and reached a kind of plateau of respectability even among the broad masses, this interest still has the aura of curiosity about it. Only a comparatively small segment of the world population truly understands the deeper meaning of living life on the esoteric level.

The theory behind the existence of soul mates goes back to the earliest history of mankind. Even in the Stone Age religion, called, appropriately, "The Old Religion," one of the prime motivations of leading a good and useful life was to be reborn again near the loved one and find the loved one again in the next incarnation. In medieval times, the idea of the divinely joined couple runs through many romantic narratives. The German poet Johann Wolfgang Goethe wrote a novel called *Die Wahlverwandtschaften*, meaning "elective affinities"—relationships by choice. It was his contention that every human being had a perfect mate (of the opposite sex) waiting to be discovered. Goethe expressed in poetic form a philosophy that is probably the deepest and most significant element of all esoteric teachings.

At the beginning, it is thought, the soul was created as an exterior expression of the Godhead, a unit unto itself, and therefore neither male nor female but both. Sometime in great antiquity the soul was split into a male and a female half and sent forth into the world to prove itself. Through testing and purification, the two halves were forever striving to reunite again. In the process, the dynamics of the world were achieved. As a result, a vastly strengthened and purified double soul would emerge to become, perhaps, what the philosopher Nietzsche called Superman.

Since the soul mates were originally part of a larger unit, they would be possessed of knowledge that need not be explained from one to the other. Consequently, one of the earmarks of finding the true soul mate was immediate recognition, instant understanding and communication beyond logical explanation, even beyond telepathy, accompanied by deep feelings of mutual love. The longing of one soul mate for the other is, in the eyes of the esoteric, the major driving force that makes man search the universe for fulfillment. Only by reaching out to this ideal soul mate can he hope to accomplish his destiny. It does not follow that everyone of us finds the soul mate destined for him or her, but the act of reaching toward it is the important thing. By that very longing, the dynamic force of motivated desire is set into motion, and the multitude of such desires creates the power reservoir whence creative people obtain their inspirations and driving force.

Soul mates are not only physically attuned to each other and, consequently, perfect for each other in the sexual sense, but they share mutual interests, have identical outlooks on all phases of life, and are in every respect compatible with one another. Soul mates are not necessarily ideal mates in terms of contemporary standards; they may differ greatly in age, social or economic background, or even race. As a matter of fact, some soul mates may be so radically different in outer appearance that the proof of their relationship lies in overcoming their differences rather than in accentuating them. But soul mates are always one male and one female, for there is neither reference to nor tolerance of homosexuality in esoteric philosophy. This is understandable, since a plus and minus attract each other, while two pluses or two minuses accomplish the opposite.

But soul mates are by no means one of a kind. Every one of us has several potential soul mates, though he may never meet up with any of them. From the material I have investigated and the philosophies I am familiar with, it would appear that each case is different and each personality requires a different set of circumstances and number of soul mates to find his whole self again. Some individuals may do so with one perfect soul mate. Some people will find such a soul mate and actually marry that person. The majority rarely do, but those who are esoterically awake will continue to hope that someday they will meet their soul mates, even though they may be married to someone else at the time. This, of course, creates another set of problems. If they find their perfect soul mates, should they abandon their conventional mates? If they do, they may find happiness but society may condemn them. If they do not, they will live with a sense of frustration to the end of their physical days.

Those who have the potential for uniting with several soul mates in their lives—usually the leaders of this world, the creative people, those who have much to give to the world—find one or several of these potential soul mates as they move through the years. For them to deny themselves the opportunity to unite with them, if only for a limited period of time, would cut off the free flow of the very energies they need to continue their mission on earth.

One has to be sure that the member of the opposite sex one has met is truly a soul mate, and that physical desires do not create a mirage. Many are the tests by which a true soul mate can be recognized. Above all, comparison of previously held knowledge about a number of subjects, possibly the question of whether both soul mates felt identical reactions toward each other at the same time, and possible reincarnation memories should all be taken into consideration before a conclusion is reached. On the other hand, conventional social, moral, and religious considerations should be carefully avoided in judging such a relationship. Frequently, the very point of such an unusual relationship is that it must be *outside* convention. In overcoming one's fears of conventionality, one earns the right to unite with the other soul mate. If it is a question of a number of soul mates during a lifetime, both partners should realize that the union may be of a limited duration for a purpose: Once that which was meant to be accomplished by their coming together again has been completed, they must each go their separate ways to unite with other respective soul mates to accomplish still other purposes meant for them as a means of fulfilling their destiny.

At times, a couple becomes involved one with the other without realizing that they are actually soul mates. In the course of time, they discover that their relationship was not merely a physical or spiritual or emotional one but develops beyond the usual elements into a deeper relationship, and one day they discover that they are soul mates and stem from a common course. In such cases, of course, it may well be that the couple stays together to the end of their earthly lives, no longer seeking other soul mates. In realizing that each individual may have more than one perfect soul mate to merge with, we should not understand this necessarily as an invitation to a kind of esoteric polygamy but merely one of possibilities. The fact that a number of potentially equal soul mates or combinations of soul mates are in existence may also mean that a particular individual has more than one chance to merge with a perfect partner under different circumstances but with equal results. This is particularly important in cases where an unhappy love affair creates the false impression in one partner that his life's purpose has been aborted and that he will never find the same kind of love again. Remember, we are *all* unique, and at the same time, *nothing* in the universe is unique. The uniqueness of self is repeated in myriads of wondrous ways throughout the universe—equal, parallel, similar, and yet not quite the same.

Let us assume that two people meet, both of them not free in the conventional sense, and that they discover a deep longing for each other, far beyond physical or emotional desire. If they are esoterically inclined, they may discover that they are soul mates. To become one, a perfect union on all levels—physical, mental, and spiritual—is not a question of indulging themselves. The joy of such unions lies not in recognizing their previous relationship but in implementing the opportunity that so patently has come their way for a reason. They cannot afford to overlook the opportunity, to offend fate. They not only have the chance to unite again as they were once united, they have the sacred duty to do so in order to recharge their energies for further accomplishments in tune with the *patterns of destiny*. Avoiding such relationships leads to individual unhappiness and surely will cause the two potential soul mates to slow their progress. Furthermore, they will each and individually face a parallel situation again at some time in the future, whether in the same incarnation or in the next one, and will again be tested as to their responsibilities and the maturity of their decisions. It is therefore inescapable that when such conditions are recognized as cases of soul mates, direct and positive action be taken by both partners to fulfill the manifest desire of destiny.